FIELDS ELYSIAN

FIELDS ELYSIAN

a portrait of hunting society

Simon Blow

J. M. Dent & Sons Ltd
London and Melbourne

First published 1983

This book is set in 12/14 Monophoto Van Dijck by
Jolly & Barber Ltd, Rugby
Printed in Italy by
International Publishing Enterprises s.r.l., Rome, for
J. M. Dent & Sons Ltd
Aldine House, 33 Welbeck Street, London W1M 8LX

British Library Cataloguing in Publication Data

Blow, Simon
    Fields elysian: a portrait of hunting society.
    1. Fox-hunting—History
    I. Title
    799.2′59′74442   SK285

ISBN 0-460-04534-2

Contents

Acknowledgments

I would like to express my gratitude to the following either for their loan of photographs or for supplying me with information during the writing of the book: Mr Denis Aldridge, the Hon. David Astor, Lord Astor, Col. Jock Atkins, the Duke of Beaufort, Lord Belper, Mr John Berkeley, Mr Anthony & Lady Jane Bethell, Miss Sybil Burnaby, Lord and Lady de Clifford, Lord Daresbury, Sir William Dugdale, Lord Egremont, Mr Michael Farrin, the Countess of Feversham, the Countess Fitzwilliam, Mr Peter Freckingham, The George Garland Collection, Mrs Sheila Gee, the Hon. Mrs Edward Greenall, Mr Anthony Hart (Secretary, The Masters of Foxhounds Association), Mr Bruce Hobbs, Miss Hermione Hobhouse, the Hon. Diana Holland-Hibbert, Mr John F. Hughes, Mr Gervase Jackson-Stops, Mr Frank Johnson, the Hon. Lady & Sir John King, Lord Knutsford, Mrs Nancy Lancaster, Mr David Laws, Mr James Lowther, Lady Dorothy Lygon, Miss Elizabeth Manners, the Duke of Marlborough, Mr Jim Meads, Lord Middleton, Mr Ferdinand Mount, Lieut-Col. Sir John Miller, Colonel G. A. Murray-Smith, Mrs Ulrica Murray-Smith, Mr Richard Spencer, the Duke of Northumberland, Mr John Nutting, Lord Parmoor, Count Guy de Pelet, the Hon. Lady Rowley, Lady Sibell Rowley, the Duke of Rutland, Col. Adrian Scrope, Miss Monica Sheriffe, Mr Hugh Sidebottom, Sir Tatton Sykes, Dinah, Lady Tollemache, Mr Peter Townend, Mr Frank Tuohy, the Hon. David Verney, Mr & Mrs Hamish Wallace, Capt. Ronnie Wallace, Mr Jim Webster, Mr & Mrs Noel Wild, Mr Dorian Williams, Lord Willoughby de Broke, the Hon. Mrs Reginald Winn, and the Earl of Yarborough.

Finally, I would like to thank Graham Bush for the care he has taken in reproducing these photographs from their originals.

For Aunt Phyllis

Not for the lust of the killing, not for the place of pride,
Not for the hate of the hunted we English saddle and ride,
But because the gift of our fathers, the blood in our veins that flows,
Must answer for ever and ever the challenge of 'Yonder he goes!'

W. H. OGILVIE

Yes, four of us only! but is it a vision?
Dear lost ones, how came ye with mortals to mix?
Me thought that ye hunted the pastures Elysian,
And between us there rolled the unjumpable Styx!

W. BROMLEY-DAVENPORT

1

Remembering Ragdale

Aunt Phyllis and Uncle Philip lived in the heart of the Quorn Country – that is to say, near Six Hills in Leicestershire. To stay at Ragdale with Aunt Phyllis, as I used to in my school holidays, was to enter a universe that was secure and impregnable against the vicissitudes of time. At Ragdale it was impossible to believe that an empire was slipping away, or that not too far distant the industrial Midlands was inching forwards its tentacles to form a vast suburbia. For the horizon at Ragdale led only to grass and beyond the dip at the end of park there was nothing more than the hamlet which was Ragdale village. From its one shop we bought our bottles of Tizer and boxes of Smarties. Ragdale was so safe, and so dependable, that I could not imagine it otherwise.

In appearance Ragdale was eccentric. Once it had been a handsome Georgian seat with a rounded portico of pillars and a composed façade of regular sash-windows. Towards the end of the last century Uncle Philip's father decided to turn Ragdale into a castellated fantasia. Red-brick battlements made up the walls and rising asymmetrically from one side of the roof was a turretted clock tower. The final touch was a very mock moat which ran halfway round the front of the house. But it was hard to discern what exactly these fake fortifications were intended to convey, so unreal did the mediaevalisms remain. As a child I thought of it as a large toy fort where I might play for ever and ever.

My first recall of Ragdale is after the Second World War, but it had not left an earlier epoch. My aunt had grown to womanhood in the reign of King Edward VII and that era of confidence and calm was stamped everywhere in the house. I felt it in the dark, pseudo-Jacobean furniture, in the row upon row of hunting prints which lined the passages, and in the photographs of family and friends which stared from sofa tables and the tops of high chests – photographs of men with pointed beards resembling King Edward and women with porcelain complexions and pearls. There was one of Lord Lonsdale signed, 'With best wishes from an ace.' And I remember one of my grandfather – Aunt Phyllis's brother – dressed in his ceremonial uniform

Ragdale Hall, near Six Hills in Leicestershire — the hunting seat of the Cantrell-Hubberstys.

as an officer in the 2nd Life Guards; also one of a young man in plus-fours and a Norfolk jacket with a terrier on his lap.

That young man in plus-fours was called Victor Conyngham. Aunt Phyllis always kept this picture on her dressing table opposite a photograph of her husband. Victor was the man she loved and would have married, but he had died of pneumonia during the First World War. Had things been different, she would have lived in the more credible Gothick fantasy of Slane Castle in Ireland, and been the Marchioness of Conyngham. Instead she married Philip Cantrell-Hubbersty. Uncle Philip was, she told me, second choice, and although she was devoted to him, it was by no means a love match. Yet they made a perfect county pair. His passion was foxhunting whilst Aunt Phyllis opened bazaars, sat on the Bench, and performed good works throughout the neighbourhood.

To an older generation, Uncle Philip remains a legend to this day in Leicestershire. He was considered the best man across grass of his period and equal to the boldest of all time. Wherever hounds were, Cantrell-Hubbersty was there. Cantrell-Hubbersty, they say, was 'unbeatable'. He hunted four to five days a week and he knew every covert, every field and every fence. But it was not only for his riding

An example of Aunt Phyllis's high spirits.

Uncle Philip (left) judging the hunters at the Fernie Horse Show with Mr H. J. Bonner in 1935.

A Quorn point-to-point during the 1920s. Left to right: Uncle Philip, the Hon. Mrs Gilbert Greenall, Aunt Phyllis, and two friends.

that Uncle Philip had earned the respect of the hunting community. During the lean years of the Second World War, when hunting was so severely under threat, he had taken over the Mastership of the Quorn hounds and seen them through. For that, he was a hunting hero.

I can still see Uncle Philip as he was in the last years of his life. Exercising his hunter, he would ride through the farm outbuildings and cry, 'Make way for the mare! Make way for the mare!' My brother and I would scatter from our romps for fear of his wrath. When dismounted, Uncle Philip walked with a stoop, and legs bowed from a lifetime's hunting. His hands had turned arthritic and his fingers had been left curled in the shape of one holding reins. I do not remember many other words, for his speech was usually restrained to a series of grunts.

Hunting was the meaning of existence to Uncle Philip and I was amazed when I learnt that he and Aunt Phyllis had once been abroad together. They had gone for their honeymoon to Venice. Had he then glimpsed the splendours of the Doge's Palace or idled in a gondola along the Grand Canal? My expectations rose and were dashed. Unused to the heat, Uncle Philip had lasted only two days before an attack of sunstroke confined him for the remainder of the honeymoon to his bed in the Danielli.

Ragdale, therefore, was a hunting country house. Frequently the Quorn met there and often I would see the hounds running across the land. I grew accustomed

During the Second World War Aunt Phyllis ran a Red Cross shop in Melton, and the stores were kept at Ragdale.

to the sight of scarlet and black coats, shining silk hats and charging hunters. It seemed strange in summer when this sport did not occur and the sound of the huntsman's horn winding from coverts was replaced by the cawing of rooks in the tall trees. I became nostalgic for the colourful hunting scene and, after Uncle Philip's death, I liked to wander to the disused room where his top hats were stretched across the floor like a severed concertina and his scarlet coats were piled, gathering

The Quorn meet at Ragdale in the 1950s. Left to right: George Barker, the Quorn huntsman since 1929, with Aunt Phyllis, M. F. H. – the Quorn's first woman Master.

must. In those long summer evenings as I lay in bed I listened to the rooks, but in my imagination I saw Uncle Philip and the hounds, and heard the horn.

For quite suddenly out hunting, Uncle Philip had fallen from his horse and died. His death was exactly as he would have wanted it. My aunt was taking the waters in Italy at the time and as she did not hold with funerals, she did not return, though she sent a wreath. The funeral, however, was a traditional hunting one. The Quorn hunt servants came in their scarlet. As the coffin was lowered to the ground, George Barker, the Quorn huntsman, blew on his horn the Gone to Ground, followed by the Gone Away, took off his cap and said, 'Goodbye, Sir.'

My aunt lived on at Ragdale and although she herself had long since ceased to ride, she succeeded her husband in the Mastership. She was the first woman Master the Quorn had had. That she accepted the responsibilities without the pleasure of hunting herself, stemmed from her strong sense of local duty. But Aunt Phyllis was not limited in outlook through her secure existence at Ragdale. She was aware that the world was likely to be quite a different place for my brother and myself. She knew that an age was drawing to its close and that change and uncertainty lay ahead. Thus we were always instructed to make our own beds in the morning. 'There won't be anybody to look after you when you grow up,' she would say in her slight, high-pitched voice.

The house was run on a very reduced staff in those post-war years. There was Jean, who was both housekeeper and my aunt's personal maid, a cook, and a number of people who came in to clean. My aunt also had a secretary to help her with her local duties. On the farm there now worked a number of Italians who had first come as prisoners-of-war and decided to stay on. One, Luigi, became my aunt's chauffeur and head man. It was a curious mixture, the Italians and the Quorn hunt. I don't think Uncle Philip cared that much for foreigners, but Aunt Phyllis had always liked Italy. She hardly spoke a word of Italian, yet she went there every year.

A lot of hunting people had always come to see my aunt and uncle. The house was always filled with ladies in tweedy coats-and-skirts, and men in tweed, twill and large, brown brogue shoes. Their presence made Ragdale seem even more permanent for me. They enjoyed my aunt's company which was certainly easier than Uncle Philip's. For outside hunting, Uncle Philip had really had no small talk. He did not bother to address a woman unless she hunted, and did not care for a constant flow of visitors. Sometimes at meals he would say to my aunt, in front of guests, 'When are they going, Puppy?' That was their single term of endearment — calling each other 'Puppy'.

What fascinated me was the mystique which surrounded hunting life and the dedication of those who pursued it. There was, for instance, the endless preparation of kit. You had to be spotless for the meet, only to be muddied five minutes later. The boning of boots, the polishing of spurs, the cleaning of coats, brushing and smoothing of hats, and the polishing of tack — all were important rituals. Often I would sit astride the saddle-horse in the tack room and hear stories from Mr Ward, the groom, as his arms swept up and down soaping bridles and stirrup leathers. He referred to Uncle Philip as 'the Major' and had a habit of repeating his sentences. 'Very particular the Major. Yes, yes. Very particular the Major,' he would go.

In the middle of the 1950s Aunt Phyllis decided to sell Ragdale. She was well into her sixties and since she had no children and could not leave the house and estate to her heirs, she saw no point in staying. The neighbourhood was very upset to lose her — because of her many good works she was described as their 'fairy godmother'. There was a two-day sale of furniture with the house and the land sold separately. I did not fully take in what had happened until it was all over and Aunt Phyllis had moved to Sussex. It meant no more talks with Mr Ward, no more

Quorn, no more games in the cuckoo wood and no more robust and cheerful hunting faces. Ragdale, which I had trusted to be forever, had gone.

But in fact Aunt Phyllis's house in Sussex turned out to be not so far removed. Many of the familiar pieces of furniture were there, as well as the hunting prints and the photographs. Two sturdy daughters of a former well-known Quorn master, 'Chicken' Burns-Hartopp, called one day and took me to a point-to-point. Friends visited from Leicestershire and brought news of Ragdale. It was now a country club, but the park had been ploughed and the tall trees where the rooks cawed had been cut down. What survived of the Ragdale I had loved was in Aunt Phyllis herself.

It was some years later that she died. She was buried in the churchyard at Ragdale next to Uncle Philip. Today they both lie under the sundial which she had found as a stone for him. Uncle Philip's sundial tombstone was an example of Aunt Phyllis's practical side. 'We'll always be able to tell the time by him, you see,' she had said with a little laugh. But with Aunt Phyllis dead, my close link with one who had grown up in the flourish of Empire was over. Through her life as a dutiful country lady I had seen the best of its standards. She had wanted to impart those standards to us. In an altered world I cannot say that I have been able to live up to them, but I was thankful not to have missed her.

After her death, I came across a collection of her photographs. They were mostly photographs of the 1920s and '30s, and mostly concerned hunting. There was a happiness, a confidence, and a certainty about the photographs – an outlook in the people that I saw as reflecting so much of my aunt's own make-up. I picked out several faces that I recognised from later Ragdale days, for that spell of my childhood had never left my mind. As Ragdale and my aunt became increasingly a memory, I realised that there must be, in other sporting country-houses, albums and assortments of photographs that would describe the unity of that singular way of life. A book could be written and illustrated which would show how foxhunting had not only penetrated the countryside, but created its own independent values across a section of society varied enough to deserve treatment as a whole. By the photographs I hoped it might be possible for a larger audience to understand that confidence and cheerfulness which could give such security to a child. In my text I would try to explain the values which bound that society.

The result is this book. In the writing and researching of it, my belief that a composite hunting community continued to exist was confirmed. Over the years it has undergone change, and these changes are narrated in the book. The pressures on hunting have been many, but hunting people have not lost their identity. Their innate cheerfulness has not gone, and they still live by their own calendar and their own code. That there remains this distinct community, as England's country-houses are emptied to museums, and the countryside either sliced by motorways or swallowed by encroaching towns, is, in itself, remarkable.

2

The Golden Age

It is an irony that the Golden Age of foxhunting should have dawned in an agricultural depression. The causes of the 1870s depression were manifold. To simplify, a period of rapid industrial expansion had falsely stimulated the demand for grain. With new industries and increased employment consumption had risen, but the farmers had not counted on a sudden inflationary decline. The result was over-production. This was followed by bad summers bringing poor harvests and then a flood of imported corn from America. Gradually, the farmers reverted to beef and dairy. Between 1870 and 1900 4,000,000 acres of arable in England and Wales were to go back to pasture. But for the foxhunter the omen was good. To ride unhindered over grass was the hunting man's dream.

Foxhunting, as we recognise it, had its origins with the seventeenth-century squirearchy. But it was different then. The idea that you could have a nice gallop across country had not occurred to them. They hunted their fox in the early morning — around 4 am — before he had digested his night meal and could not run. It was mainly slow, woodland hunting. Then Hugo Meynell, the son of a Derbyshire squire, saw that if you hunted the fox in full daylight he would run. It was surely more enjoyable to hunt a fox at speed and so he started to breed hounds to that effect. In the 1750s Meynell moved down to the fast grass country of Leicestershire. He established himself at Quorn Hall, Quorndon, and was the first Master of that pack to appreciate the great potential of the rolling grassland.

From Quorn Hall Hugo Meynell set the precedent for the new type of hunting. He was Master of the Quorn for forty-seven years and his famous Mastership caught the attention of those in fashionable society. He invented the winter hunting season for them, and to Quorn Hall they flocked. Previously squires may have hunted, but the civilised man of fashion and letters considered it an occupation for dim rustics. Meynell altered this. A friend of Dr Johnson and Horace Walpole, he had a dry wit and was known in the London drawing-rooms. If Meynell did it, there must be something to it, and soon London society was hunting with him.

Along with the grand tour, foxhunting became a part of the English gentleman's education. In Yorkshire, Sir Mark Masterman Sykes was filling an outstanding library whilst at the same time designing the hunt buttons for his pack. In Sussex, the third Earl of Egremont was lodging Turner, patronizing the arts and acquiring a pack of hounds. But equally there were single-minded characters who have become legends in the annals of the sport, such as George Osbaldeston, the demented Jack Mytton and Tom Assheton-Smith. Both Osbaldeston and Mytton ruined themselves for sport, although Mytton's downfall and retreat to Calais was more dramatic than Osbaldeston's retrenchment to St John's Wood. But they were men of the Regency and their excesses not out of keeping.

The first Golden Age of hunting began with Hugo Meynell and continued through to the 1850s. There were cries of alarm that the advent of railways would

Richard Greville Verney, 19th Baron Willoughby de Broke, playing with his dog. Like his father before him, Willoughby de Broke was Master of the Warwickshire, a great foxhunter and upholder of the county tradition.

The first brush for the small son of a tenant farmer on the Fitzwilliam estate at Milton, near Peterborough.

interrupt the scent and bring too many 'foreigners' out. But hunting was not drastically changed and, if anything, the railways were to prove beneficial. With an agricultural depression approaching, it would be less easy to continue the tradition of the squire maintaining a pack for himself, the neighbours and the farmers. Visitors could help the hunt funds by paying either a subscription or a 'cap' per day hunted. Also, as the rich industrialists came to support hunting, they needed quick exit routes if they were to attend to their affairs.

By the 1870s foxhunting had taken its place on the country-house timetable. After public school, the sons of landed families progressed naturally to either Oxford or Cambridge. Once there, scholarship was not made a necessity for them. Even if they were younger sons it was unlikely that they would have to earn their livelihoods strenuously. The experience of Lord Willoughby de Broke must have been typical of many freshmen. His tutor had impressed upon him the pleasures of learning, and mildly suggested it as a duty for one who might have responsibilities later. But there arose a conflict in Willoughby de Broke's mind. 'It would mean reading seven

The Fitzwilliam huntsman holds up the masks of a brace of foxes — trophies of the day's sport.

Atherstone Hunt puppy walkers. Hound puppies are born in March and April and 'walked' until the following January when they return to the kennels. Yeomen and tenant farmers and their sons make up this body of hunting enthusiasts of the early 1900s.

hours a day, including attendance at lectures,' he pondered. 'How was I to hunt if I were to read seven hours a day?' With a stableful of his father's hunters at his disposal in nearby Warwickshire and horses waiting for him there in Oxford, it must be no surprise that hunting won the day.

Lord Willoughby de Broke was an intelligent man. He was to play an important role as a 'Ditcher' in the House of Lords' opposition to the Liberal threat to create 500 new peers in order to enact constitutional changes. In spite of his Oxford story, Lord Willoughby de Broke was rather well read and could write himself. But coming from a county and landowning family it was hunting that was nearest his heart. Like nearly all landed families he not only enjoyed hunting, but believed it to be the backbone of country life. For hunting had broadened its status since being simply the squire's amusement. In the county hierarchy, second in importance after the Lord-Lieutenant came the Master of Foxhounds.

The structure of the county was as neat and as interlocking as a cut and laid fence. From the landowners the list ran on to the Church, to the Law, to the Army, to the MP, to the minor clergy and to the larger farmers. There was an understood place and correct manner of social exchange for everyone. The county magnates did not busy themselves with the details of the management of their estates, but stood as figureheads. They represented security and the unchanging order. And so at Eton one heir was overheard saying to another, 'Don't bother about farming or politics;

all father's tenants have to do is to walk a foxhound puppy and vote for the Conservatives.'

The unifying events which held all in a common bond were, in summer, cricket, and in winter, foxhunting. If you could not afford to ride you followed the hunt on foot or on a bicycle. The foot followers were as recognised in the pageant as those who were mounted. Often they provided invaluable services to the hunt, such as walking the hound puppies until they were ready to go to kennels. Many had followed the hunt for a lifetime and were more likely to know which way the fox was running than the young swells out for a thrill.

The social divisions were accepted and not questioned. At the lower rural levels there was poverty, but it did not compare with the slum conditions in the big cities. The healthy advantages of an outdoor life, and knowing that in a small community kindness was more forthcoming, kept people cheerful. In *Lark Rise to Candleford*, an autobiographical novel of village life at the turn of the century, Flora Thompson put it like this: 'Most of the men sang or whistled as they dug or hoed. There was a good

Villagers often followed the hunt on foot. Here one of the school children is 'blooded' by the Fitzwilliam.

Belvoir second horsemen follow the hunt with their masters' fresh mounts. The cockade top hats were standard livery in many hunting establishments.

deal of outdoor singing in those days. Workmen sang at their jobs; men with horses and carts sang on the road; the baker, the miller's man, and the fish-hawker sang as they went from door to door; even the doctor and the parson on their rounds hummed a tune between their teeth.'

For the landowner there was no shortage of stable staff. There was a stable-lad for every two horses, grooms and second horsemen. Sometimes a rough-rider would be employed to school the difficult horses. A hunting yard usually numbered not less than ten horses and if it was a large yard like the Duke of Beaufort's at Badminton or Sir Gilbert Greenall's in Rutland, the number could run to sixty or seventy. On the flying grass of the Shires – and occasionally elsewhere – you required two horses per day. It was the job of the second horseman to hack the two horses to the meet, hand one to his master, and to ride the second horse round the roads until they changed. The second horsemen were meant to follow the hunt but not take part in it. This deprivation could lead to rebellion in the ranks and then Masters were obliged to issue an order stating that second horsemen were not to 'lark over fences'.

A Master of Foxhounds had the authority to be an autocrat in the field. Depending on individual character, each Master used this authority differently. Lord Lonsdale, probably the best known hunting figure of his day, played his autocracy to the full. He was an excellent horseman but he also had an inflated ego. As a young man he had at first been relatively hard up, having an elder brother who consumed the vast income that he craved. But by chance, the elder brother died, and Hugh Lowther became Lord Lonsdale. His income increased from £1,000 a year to nearly £100,000, and at once he launched himself into the extravagances which were to earn him the title of 'the Yellow Earl'. Every servant was to be dressed, and every carriage and car painted, in the canary yellow of the Lonsdale livery. He appointed a Master of Horse, a Groom of the Bedchamber and a Master of Music for his private orchestra. Smoking his famous six-inch cigars, Lonsdale moved in a royal progress from one Lowther seat to another, his principal sporting seat being Barley Thorpe in Rutland.

It has been said that, 'the doings of the Quorn were, in hunting circles, comparable to the fate of the Government to the general public.' In 1893 Hugh Lonsdale was invited to become Master. With such a pack in his control, Lonsdale had the perfect opportunity to display both his autocracy and egotism. A first act was to institute a new hunt button. It was designed with a large coronet above and a

The Hon. Lancelot Lowther on the left, with his elder brother the Earl of Lonsdale. Lord Lonsdale was Master of the Quorn from 1893 to 1898 and of the Cottesmore from 1907 to 1911. Called the Yellow Earl, he was famous for his love of sport and spending. His brother Lancelot liked to imitate his manner and sometimes acted as his Field-Master.

patronisingly small 'Quorn' below. The hunt servants were fitted out in new liveries, swapping buckskin for white leather breeches, with Lowther buttons sewn on the dark-red coats. At Quorn meets the most noticeable carriage was the yellow landau of the Master.

Lonsdale's spending and showmanship were the talk of hunting circles. As Master of the Quorn, his behaviour could hardly pass unnoticed. And in the field he was equally autocratic. It did not take much irritation from a thrusting rider over-riding hounds to make Lonsdale announce that he was taking hounds home. He was fortunate to have in Tom Firr one of the greatest huntsmen that have ever been, but this did not prevent Lonsdale from insisting that *his* method of killing foxes be adopted. Quorn followers tended to be a hard-riding élite, and they were not used to being put down in this way. Many preferred the days when his brother, Lancelot Lowther, acted as deputy. But did not Lonsdale's trouble really stem from those twenty-five years as a younger brother? His extravagances, his ego and his auto-cracy were his ways of getting even.

However, not all were despots on the lines of Lord Lonsdale. The landowning Masters practised a benevolent despotism which was expected and admired. In North Wales the family of Williams-Wynn owned almost the entire country they hunted over. Since the creation of their baronetcy in the seventeenth century nearly every holder had borne the christian name Watkin. The size of their estates is indicated by the occasion when the 6th Baronet was interrogated during a train journey as to the ownership of various passing farms. The answer was always, 'Me'. When this Sir Watkin rode through the villages the children would rally and cry, 'Sir Watkin for ever!' He reigned at the Williams-Wynn seat of Wynnstay until his death in 1885. He kennelled the hounds there, paid for all the hunt's outgoings, and hunted it as a private pack. 'Old Wattie', as his friends called him, was something of a lovable local monument. Out hunting, he could be recognised from afar because he usually rode with his red coat unbuttoned, a bandana handkerchief stretching from his pocket to his mouth, and holding his whip by the thong so that it waved wildly behind him.

The hunting landowner believed firmly in tradition, and few were Whigs or cared for radicalism. Hunting is dependent on a respect for country values, and on the changelessness of the county structure. The Tory squires had a horror of the cities with their labour movements and spirit of unrest. 'Compton Verney,' reflected Lord Willoughby de Broke, 'was too close to Birmingham to be pleasant for a peer.' They loathed Radicals like Cobden and Bright whom they saw as little better than revolutionaries. The Radicals and the Liberals were to blame for the Reform Bill, the Repeal of the Corn Laws and the Second Reform Bill of 1867 which had given the vote to the working man. With no knowledge of the laws of the countryside, the Radicals were destroying the ancient and time-honoured principles by which it functioned. The passing of these Bills had contributed to the agricultural depression

The Earl of Harrington took over the South Notts. in 1882 and renamed the hunt the Earl of Harrington's. He financed the whole pack himself and carried the horn until his death in 1917.

which was forcing some of the smaller squires to sell up. Where would it end?

At night, in mahogany and candle-lit dining rooms, just such a discussion continued over the port. And there was always one who would need no prompting to recite the prophecy of that beloved foxhunting Member of Parliament, Walter Bromley-Davenport:

> For I looked into its pages, and I read the book of fate,
> And saw foxhunting abolished by an order of the State;
>
> Saw the heavens filled with guano, and the clouds at men's command
> Raining down unsavoury liquids for the benefit of land;
>
> Saw the airy navies earthwards bear the planetary swell,
> And the long projected railroad made from Halifax to H–l;
>
> Saw the landlords yield their acres after centuries of wrongs,
> Cotton lords turn country gentlemen in patriotic throngs;
>
> Queen, religion, State abandoned, and the flags of party furled
> In the Government of Cobden, and the dotage of the world.

There was a division, too, between the Tory landowners and those reared in the great Whig houses to back reform. T. F. Dale writing the story of a foxhunting leader, the 8th Duke of Beaufort, stated that 'the Russells and the Cavendishes diligently sawed off the main branches of the political tree on which they sat.' When Lord Dalmeny, the son of the Liberal Prime Minister, Lord Rosebery, came out for a day with the Belvoir he was told by the Master's wife, Lady Greenall, 'We don't want your kind out with us!' But the Whig dynasties had grown up in an atmosphere of political and intellectual exchange of ideas. They could appreciate that other worlds existed that were very different from their own. Support of radical dissension had made them aware that the concept of the noble seat and its estate belonged to a privileged minority. The sensibilities of the foxhunting Tory landowner did not stretch that far. He might be thoughtful and often munificent towards his tenants and employees, but he had no doubts about the hereditary principle.

The Whig families were not noticeably ardent foxhunters in this Golden Age — with one exception. At Althorp in Northamptonshire, the 5th Earl Spencer led a double life. His career in public office had begun when he was returned as a Liberal in 1857. He went on to be Viceroy of Ireland and to hold various posts in Gladstone's administrations, but throughout these commitments he remained a passionate foxhunter and was thrice Master of the Pytchley. 'There is nothing like a good gallop across country to drive dull care away,' he remarked when trouble in Ireland was dogging his peace.

Lord Spencer always had a sympathy for the underdog, and although his nickname 'The Red Earl' was chiefly on account of a flowing red beard, it could cut two ways. At Althorp the Red Earl busied himself with the care and maintenance of the Pytchley pack, often hunting the hounds himself and keeping a detailed journal. In London he maintained an unflagging loyalty to Gladstone – the man whom most of Lord Spencer's neighbours regarded as the Arch Demon. When Gladstone introduced the Home Rule Bill for Ireland in the 1880s it split the Liberal Party. To give Ireland independence was contrary to the very achievements of the British Empire and to undermine its strength. Most of the leading Whigs who until then had shaped Liberal policy, refused to serve. Only a handful of Whig peers stuck by Gladstone, and one was Lord Spencer. Society was dismayed and puzzled by the Red Earl's adherence. Sir Dighton Probyn, a member of the Prince of Wales's Household, exclaimed, 'A man of that sort advocating Communism shakes my belief in anything mortal.'

For his great service to the chase, however, the hunting fraternity could not judge Lord Spencer too harshly. Also, like other large landowners, he had not been immune from the effects of the depression. With few rents coming in, he had been

The select team of gentleman cricketers known as I Zingari. In the summer those who hunted often turned to cricket as a pastime. Several members of the I Zingari team were keen foxhunters. Second from the left in the front row is Bay Middleton – the paramour and pilot of the Empress Elizabeth of Austria.

obliged to sell his library in order to keep the house in repair and avoid diminishing the estate. A part of the money fetched had further gone to paying for the hounds. The Pytchley overlooked his entertaining Gladstone and remembered instead the hospitality he had extended to the Empress of Austria.

It was through Lord Spencer that Elizabeth of Austria had come to the Pytchley and there found her pilot and paramour, Bay Middleton. Tired of the restrictions of Austrian Court life, the Empress had heard of the flying grass countries of England. She was an enthusiastic horsewoman and there was no comparable hunting at home. Whilst renting her first hunting-box, Easton Neston, and hunting with the Grafton, Lord Spencer had encouraged her to try his pack, the Pytchley. The Grafton country round Easton Neston was known for its large, bullfinch fences, but it rode heavy and did not have the light galloping grass of the Pytchley. Determined to leave her mark in the toughest of hunting countries, the Empress was easily persuaded. In the hall at Althorp before the meet, she was introduced to Captain Middleton.

Bay Middleton was the ideal of the sporting gentleman of that time. Born to a hunting background, he held a commission in the 12th Lancers and through his reputation in the hunting field he had been specially selected to be a 'hunting' ADC to Lord Spencer in Ireland. The post was created in an attempt to ensure a measure of protection for the Red Earl who insisted on hunting when Irish unrest was putting the lives of British dignitaries in danger. Middleton's commanding officer was not unhappy to see him go; he had a habit of blowing calls on his hunting horn while his senior was taking an afternoon nap. The hunting fields had many like Bay Middleton: hard-riding and high-spirited cavalry men who would stop at nothing and enjoyed a good practical joke. But Middleton also had that indefinable charm which the upper classes can be so adept at breeding.

The daring pace of the hunting Empress and her closeness to Middleton were the talk of the sporting drawing rooms. For the season of 1878–9 she rented Cottesbrooke Park which lay within a short distance of Althorp. Lord Spencer had found her the house and there was a constant exchange of dinner parties between the two houses with Middleton always in attendance. During the day it was hunting with her now dear friend Spencer as Master, and Middleton as pilot. For her elegance, beauty and bravery she was widely admired, but in official circles she showed a want of tact. Her dislike of Court duties made her flaunt the Queen's hospitality. When she did finally condescend to visit Windsor, Queen Victoria noted with a certain acidity in her diary, 'She spoke with delight of having hunted each day since she arrived!!'

The Empress of Austria had set a precedence in 'society' for ladies of fashion to hunt again. In the early nineteenth century a prejudice had developed against women hunting. This had not been the case in previous centuries. But in the nineteenth century a woman hunting did not fit with an attitude which decreed that ladies of position should be pale, delicate and silent. It was accepted to the point that the perfect woman in the novels of Thackeray and Dickens is drawn as a dull and unreal hot-house creature. There had been some revolt in the hunting field before the Empress, but following her example, late Victorian and Edwardian women hunted with a vengeance, as if there might be no tomorrow.

Since Hugo Meynell at Quorndon, Melton Mowbray had become the hunting centre. It was not purely fashion which dictated this but those bold thrusters — as the expression is — who wanted to ride at speed over daunting obstacles. A second attraction was that Melton was within hacking distance of three packs. From Melton you could hunt six days a week if you wished, picking from the Quorn, the Belvoir or the Cottesmore. From 1800 onwards swells, hard-riders, beauties and dissolutes had migrated to Melton for the season, and all over the town and on its outskirts lodges and hunting-boxes had sprung up.

legend, past and present. There were the stories of the who, with some chums, had literally decided to paint s from that incident that the euphemism, 'to paint the

hire attracted Edwardian Meltonians, as they had since the days of Hugo Meynell.

*Two regular Meltonians amusing themselves during a pause with the Belvoir. Major Joe
Laycock makes his horse lie down to an admiring Mr Myddleton.*

town red', derives.) There was another story of Waterford riding his hunter over a
five-bar gate in his own dining room, and another of him placing a donkey in the bed
of a stranger. There was the drunken Marquis of Hastings who, before his final ruin
through an untimely £100,000 bet in the Derby, had somehow been Master of the
Quorn for two seasons, even though he was usually too hungover while hunting to
make any sense. And more recently there was the aged Lady Cardigan, widow of the
Light Brigade Earl, who waited scantily dressed on her balcony, and heavily rouged
and painted, in the hope that a passing stablelad might take her for a comely lass.

But as much for its history of frivolity, Melton's reputation was for the quality
of its hunting. In the education of the nineteenth-century public-school boy the cult
of manliness was stressed and what better place to prove it than over the fast and
dangerous grass country? Manliness meant the ability to lead, and leadership was a
prerequisite of Empire. As the British Empire grew and spread throughout the
century, so did the number of young men trained to command. The hunting field

was the best training ground, combining pleasure with purpose. By the 1880s, therefore, Melton was a fixture on the social calendar. Moreton Frewen, a young man-about-town of the day, described his year thus: 'From November to April Melton, then a month's salmon fishing in Ireland and Punchestown; in May, June, July, London; then Goodwood and Cowes; then "grouse" somewhere and Doncaster; next a broken week or two at Newmarket and a little schooling of young Irish horses after cubs. Such as this was the determination to pleasure of tens of thousands – of really the pick of our young fellows.'

Second horses and a break for lunch in the Shires.

Hunting undergraduates from Oxford attend a college point-to-point at Stratton Audley in March 1901.

If youthful society could enjoy itself in this breezy and carefree manner, perhaps the agricultural depression had not played too much havoc with the finances of the landowning class. It had not meant indeed that their offspring would go penniless into the world, but it had meant a curbing of other expenditures. Whereas before it had been normal for a hunting landowner to hunt the pack privately, and take no subscription from the followers, his income was no longer large enough to allow for this expense. The cost of feeding at least forty couple of hounds, buying the horses for the hunt servants and paying their wages, keeping the coverts and the country in proper repair, was considerable. Money was needed for hunting if the opportunities of this halcyon epoch were not to be lost. The answer lay with the industrial magnates.

It was not always for prestige that new money was drawn to land. Admittedly most new magnates started with that reason, but they soon found themselves absorbed by country pursuits. This particularly applied to those who took to foxhunting. The Heythrop was badly requiring an injection of cash when Albert Brassey, the son of Thomas Brassey the railway contractor, appeared. He bought Heythrop Park and, through a long Mastership from 1873 to 1918, he principally paid for all the outgoings. He grew fascinated by hound-breeding and re-established the Heythrop as a pack which could hold its own with those in the Shires. So attached to his hunting was Brassey that he used to arrange the next season's meets during the summer from his yacht on the Mediterranean. Friendliness was Brassey's yardstick, and he gave a special welcome to the undergraduates from Oxford. An undergraduate who hunted there late in Brassey's Mastership said of the Heythrop, 'A lot of nice old gentlemen in long coats who don't curse you as much as they do with the Bicester.'

The old landed aristocracy might grumble about 'trade' yet none could complain of the ease with which Albert Brassey had slipped into his role of benevolent landlord. But in 1896 an even more surprising situation arose. The Duke of Rutland announced that he wished to retire from the hereditary Mastership of his hounds. There had been a pack of hounds at Belvoir since the middle of the eighteenth century and only once had the ducal Mastership been broken. Like the Quorn, the Belvoir had a unique image and of this sudden vacancy it was written, 'The position had nearly as much honour as that of Prime Minister. Many desired it, men of millions and men famous in field.' Allowing for the writer's purple, it was nonethe-

The Duke of Rutland (far right), who gave up the hereditary Mastership of his Belvoir hounds, watches a meet from the Castle walls.

In the centre wearing a grey bowler is Sir Gilbert Greenall, a rich Cheshire brewer, who succeeded the Duke of Rutland in the Mastership of the Belvoir. He is seen talking to Mr Bemrose, a local farmer, at a Belvoir Puppy Show in the 1900s.

The new Belvoir stables at Woolsthorpe in Rutland ready to hold seventy horses. They were built for Sir Gilbert Greenall in six months and used from his first season as Master in 1896.

The tack room at the new stables.

less a departure for the Mastership of the Duke of Rutland's hounds to go to the twenty-nine-year-old son of a Cheshire brewer.

That the Belvoir estate was unable to support the hounds was not the full case. The estate then was 40,000 acres, and it had an industrial income. The Duke of Rutland enjoyed politics and fishing, but not hunting. It was sensible therefore that the hounds should be cared for by a rich man and an enthusiast, and Gilbert Greenall was both. His father was a Parliamentary colleague of the Duke's, and the Duke knew of Greenall's abilities. He knew, too, of the finance required to preserve the high standards of his hunt. As witness to this, Gilbert Greenall had built, within six months' of his appointment, a splendid new yard fit to hold seventy horses. The Duke's choice was to herald a glorious era for the Belvoir. The hounds remained kennelled at Belvoir and the property of the Duke, but they were now organised and paid for by Greenall. It was yet another example of aristocratic survival by acknowledging an unstated degree of social flexibility within the code.

It was indeed fortunate when the large estates had interests elsewhere, such as coal or slate mines, or property. In Yorkshire, a redoubtable hound-breeder and foxhunter, Lord Middleton, was able to draw an income from the coal mines on his other estate, Wollaton, near Nottingham. The Dukes of Beaufort and Northumberland owned mines in Wales and England respectively. While the depression lasted, not only could the hounds be saved but rents from tenants lowered or waived. But

Most hunts held a hedge-cutting competition to encourage the proper cutting and laying of fences. Lord Annaly, Master of the Pytchley, judges his hunt's competition.

Frank Freeman, one of the outstanding huntsmen of this century, with his hounds in the Pytchley Kennels.

there were sufferers. Lord Willoughby de Broke, for instance, had found it expensive to entertain King Edward VII, and apart from land he had no other income. He was obliged to make periodic lettings of Compton Verney. One of his tenants, Sir Ernest Cassel, advised him that there could be iron ore on the estate. Willingly and immediately, the noble peer dug, but to no effect.

By the turn of the century the benefits of the industrialism once so spurned by the landed class were being enjoyed by all. The railway had meant that hounds and horses could go by train to distant meets; 'hunting specials' went from King's Cross to Melton and carried Oxford undergraduates to the Heythrop or the Warwickshire; the country-house party grew in size, and the train brought those rich, vital subscribers. The conditions of hunting had improved too. The land was better drained making it easier for galloping, and for the horse the clipping machine was a boon — hitherto, being ridden all day with a full coat was uncomfortable, being clipped with a cut-throat razor possibly worse.

Good fencing, drained fields and carefully nurtured coverts had made a hunting landscape that Hugo Meynell would have envied. His foxhound bred for speed was being hunted over perfect countryside and, with the improving techniques of hunting, there came legendary huntsmen. The names Frank Gillard, Will Dale and George Carter were among those spoken of with awe, but the two names which dominated hunting talk before 1914 were Tom Firr and Frank Freeman. For when hunting people meet in conclave, wars, revolutions and depressions are set aside: what matters is the artistry of the chase.

It was said that Frank Freeman could speak to his hounds with his eyes. He had a melancholy, distant expression and spoke little. He had been born within the sound of the cry of hounds in Kildare, where his father was huntsman. Freeman made the progression that a would-be huntsman must make through the hunt servant grades: 2nd Whipper-in to the South-West Wilts, then the Tickham, the Brocklesby and the Belvoir, then 1st Whipper-in to the Belvoir and after that the West Cheshire. Finally he became huntsman to the Bedale and, two seasons later, at the age of thirty, huntsman to the Pytchley.

Hunt service is a vocation; no hunt servant would turn down the opportunity to hunt a leading pack, but the spaces are far between. Freeman's potential had first been noticed by Henry Chaplin — a legend himself as a Tory squire — while out with the Belvoir. Freeman was deputising as huntsman that day, and he had been blowing his horn too much. 'The Squire', as Chaplin was called, gave him advice. The day progressed better and, at the end of it, Chaplin recalled, 'He was so nice and modest-minded a fellow that he came half-a-mile out of his way to meet me.' Freeman thanked him. 'The ambition of my life is to be a huntsman. I am most anxious to learn,' he said.

The Master who had selected Frank Freeman to come from Yorkshire to the Pytchley was Lord Annaly. Their association as huntsman and Master was a model

A meet of the Pytchley at Brixworth Hall in the 1900s. On the left is Henry Chaplin (later Lord Chaplin), known as 'The Squire', and on the right Lord Annaly, Master of the Pytchley from 1902 to 1914.

of its kind. Lord Annaly was an equerry and Lord-in-Waiting to the Prince of Wales, later King George V, and he had married the heiress of Holdenby House in Northamptonshire. In bearing and looks Annaly was the image of the aristocratic foxhunter and his presence alone was sufficient to command respect. Unlike Lord Lonsdale he did not need to state his authority, it was already felt. His duty was to hold back a hard-riding Pytchley field and to give Frank Freeman the freedom to hunt his hounds without tiresome interference from himself or bother from the Pytchley fashionables.

The result of the Annaly-Freeman partnership was a decade of unsurpassed sport. Frank Freeman's dedication was such that he would never accept a lift back to the kennels after a tough day or in bad weather. 'I'd rather go home with my hounds; they wouldn't go home without me,' was his reply. And sometimes this would mean fifteen miles in an open horse-drawn van. As the huntsman of a 'smart' pack showing an excellence of exciting runs and foxes killed, he became natural prey for flattery. A fashionable field – preferring the fast pace to learning about hounds at work – rarely grasped that the huntsman has a task. It was well summed up for Freeman one day when a rich follower presented him with an ornate gold whip for which he had no use. 'I'd rather he get off and help sometimes. I believe he lost me the fox the other day. Them! They're no use to me; I never use them,' Freeman muttered.

A life in hunt service was understood by a good Master of Foxhounds, and understood too by those interested in the science of hunting and what lay behind the performance. Apart from those who hunted to ride, there was a body of men who lived for the science, which was dominated by hound breeding. The traditional English foxhound descended from those hounds bred by Meynell and his contemporaries, and in the blood line would be Mr Barry's 'Bluecap', Mr Corbet's 'Trojan', and from the Brocklesby the famous 'Rallywood'. There were the 'governing' kennels whose business it was to keep the strains pure and aimed at perfection — the Beaufort, the Fitzwilliam, the Belvoir, the Warwickshire and the Brocklesby. And in 1878 the Peterborough Hound Show had started, where prizes were awarded for the hound which attained the ideal.

A Kennel Stud-Book was instituted and its compilation was carried out by the Reverend Cecil Legard. Legard was a hunting parson but he was better known for

The hound van used during Frank Freeman's pre-war period as huntsman. He always drove home on it, whatever the weather; he liked to be near his hounds as much as possible.

The Reverend Cecil Legard, dressed in his customary Regency style, judging the Belvoir Puppy Show in 1911. With him is George Leafe, the huntsman of the Quorn.

his knowledge of hounds than for his bravery in the chase. He had left his native Yorkshire to be vicar of Cottesbrooke in Northamptonshire and since Jane Austen had based *Mansfield Park* on Cottesbrooke, he found the Regency a more agreeable period than his own. His dress was a frock coat, winged collar, tight-fitting trousers and a tall top hat. Legard wrote and spoke an antique English and his profound judgment of a hound could only be swayed by a different opinion from a peer. The importance of the person he was addressing could be measured by the straightening of his back. His weakness for a title was thought strange since his brother was a twelfth baronet, but Legard could not cure himself. He once left two farmers in a railway compartment on the pretext that he disliked smoking, only to join two peers puffing at cigars. At the next stop, one of the farmers interjected drily through the window, 'I see the smoke of the lord is savoury to the priest's nostrils.'

The Peterborough Hound Show, 1889. On the left is Will Goodall, huntsman to the Pytchley. In the centre wearing a white kennel-coat is Merthyr Guest, autocratic and legendary Master of the Blackmore Vale.

Some of the eighty hunters stabled by Merthyr Guest at Inwood. Guest and the hunt servants rode only greys, and while he was Master, the Blackmore Vale hunted six days a week.

Huntsmen, whippers-in and second horsemen to the Blackmore Vale during the Mastership of Merthyr Guest.

Hunting absorbed eccentrics and originals; if anything they fitted well with a contrariness in country life. Down in the south-west of England was Merthyr Guest, a tall, bushy-bearded and cadaverous man, who for sixteen years dominated the Blackmore Vale. He was another autocrat who had benefited by a marriage to a rich woman. Lady Theodora Guest was a favourite daughter of the Marchioness of Westminster, whose wedding present to her daughter and son-in-law was a large house and estate. From Inwood House in Somerset, Merthyr and Lady Theodora ran the hunt on a princely scale and visitors came from afar for a day with the Blackmore Vale. During Guest's reign it even outshone the Shires for lavishness. At Inwood he kennelled one hundred couple of hounds and kept a stable of eight hunters, all greys. He took no subscription whatsoever and hunted his hounds six days a week. A less lavish side, however, to Merthyr Guest was his strict teetotalism. When on a cold day his hunt servants were suddenly hopeful as he stopped at a public house, he merely tipped the whiskies down their boots to keep their feet warm. But an eccentric autocracy finally ruled him. He resigned the Mastership in 1900 and offered his prize-winning bred pack to his successors, but stipulating unacceptable conditions. The hounds were never to have their ears rounded,

The Marquess of Worcester (later the 10th Duke of Beaufort), aged 9, with his own pack of harriers which were given to him on his ninth birthday by his father. Ever since then he has been called 'Master' by his friends.

*The Beaufort meet in the park at Badminton in 1909. The photograph was taken by the
Dowager Empress of Russia who was staying at Badminton with her sister
Queen Alexandra (on the right of the picture).*

*Lady Blanche and Lady Diana Somerset out with their father's hounds at
Badminton, January 1910.*

The Marquess of Worcester, Master of Harriers, with his father the 9th Duke of Beaufort,
M. F. H., on the steps at Badminton, 1910.

Lord Middleton's hounds meet at Sledmere House, Yorkshire, in 1911, a few months after the house had been gutted by fire. Lord Middleton was a noted hound-breeder and his wife, Lady Middleton, is on the far right.

branded — most packs carry this identification — or to have their dew-claws cut. The rounding of ears was common practice then and most hounds had their dew-claws cut to prevent them being broken. But to these possessive provisos the committee would not agree. Merthyr Guest therefore sold his hounds out of the country and it was to be some years before the Blackmore Vale recovered its strength. Yet Guest was indifferent, and he retired to Inwood to occupy himself with science and biology.

Throughout England were spread the hunting country houses, committed to the breeding of hounds and maintaining of standards. At Brocklesby Park there was Lord Yarborough, whose family had owned the hounds in unbroken line since the eighteenth century. On every tenant's lease the customary requests were made: to permit the hunt access, to take down wire, and to walk a foxhound puppy. At Badminton there was the Duke of Beaufort, each Duke continuing to be a sporting landowner and encouraging the hunting of the vast terrain that went with it. The young Somersets had foxhunting set in their blood ahead of speech: 'We are not allowed to hunt more than three times a week till we are five years old,' said one of them. At Lord Middleton's Yorkshire seat, Birdsall, there were horses and hounds bred with particular reference to negotiating the Wold landscape. And so it was in many other places, a self-sufficient universe unheeding of external events.

When not hunting, Lady Middleton liked to ride her ass, Mombassa, a gift from an African potentate. Apart from Birdsall in Yorkshire, the Middletons had another seat at Wollaton, near Nottingham. The ass usually accompanied Lady Middleton when they moved seats. Here she is seen at Wollaton.

The arrival of the motor car was not viewed kindly in hunting circles. It could head a fox or interrupt the scent. None the less, it soon gained in appeal. Left to right: Lady Violet Charteris, Lady Lytton and Lady Diana Manners prepare to leave for the meet from Belvoir. On the steps is Lady Lytton's son, Lord Knebworth.

The motor enclosure at the Pytchley point-to-point in 1911.

*Stable-lads in the early 1900s take the opportunity to ride Mr George Fitzwilliam's hunter
back to the stable yard at Milton after a morning's cub-hunting.*

But an alarm was raised in the 1900s with the arrival of the motor car. Was this further invasion from the machine age now going to curtail the peace and harmony of the magical moment? The railway had been passed as bearable, and looked on logically as beneficial, but the car would mean a multitude of new roads, it could run anywhere. Lord Willoughby de Broke, always ready to contest a threat to the stabilised order, argued its necessity with a dry humour:

> The most plausible defence of hunting by motor car is that the time saved in this manner can be profitably devoted to the transaction of business, domestic or otherwise. When people say this, they probably mean lying in bed. But granted that the busy man can leave the door at 10.15 a.m. in a motor car instead of at 9.30 a.m. in a carriage, is there much real saving of tissue? The time spent between 9.30 a.m. and 10.15 a.m. might be more restfully spent in the phaeton or the buggy than talking on the telephone, interviewing the agent, or composing letters to creditors.

The interference of the car was not a false alarm, and the Masters of Foxhounds took up their grievance in common voice. *Baily's Hunting Directory* was the vital and perused annual of the hunting man. It listed every pack of hounds in England, Wales, Scotland and Ireland, abroad and in the outposts of Empire. It indicated the type of horse required for the different hunting countries, stated the amount of subscription, the lie of the country and the days of meeting. The *Directory* gave advice to beginners on behaviour in the field and on the cleaning of hunting clothes. There was a listing of 'hotels for sportsmen' and no aspect of the foxhunters' needs was neglected. Now, after the 'Days of Meeting', came the admonition for nearly every pack: 'It is requested that motors be sent straight home from the meet, and in no case allowed to follow hounds.'

Yet the golden age was not seriously interrupted, for the car was in in its infancy and numbers of country families continued to use the buggy, especially those families who restricted their travelling to the meet, the point-to-point, and nearby friends. It was in these houses that a devotion to hunting was made clear, both inside and outside. In the stables would be the grooms, stable-boys, horses for the family and their guests, and ponies for the children. For like the Somersets, the children were taught to ride before their first teeth had grown. Inside the house the hunting atmosphere was as redolent as in the stables: the hunting crops hanging in the hall; the line-up of boots in the boot-room; the oil paintings of hunters in full flight or standing, ears pointed, in the stable with an attendant groom; the coloured prints of hunting scenes and the steeplechase; the hunting cartoons with their funny captions; and in the library, the novels of Whyte, Melville, Surtees and Trollope.

The young men shaped by this background were going either to the army or to Oxford or Cambridge, as their predecessors had done. The House — as Christ Church

Basil Nightingale, the horse artist, painting at Inwood for Merthyr and Lady Theodora Guest in 1892.

*The Master and three whippers-in of the Oxford University Drag in.1901. Back row:
H. R. Pape, L. H. Hardy, and D. K. Courage. Centre: Waldorf Astor, the Master.*

was familiarly known — was taking in hunting heirs and younger sons just as in
Squire Chaplin's day. 'You seem to regard Christ Church as a hunting box,' the
Dean had informed him, and it had not altered. For the sporting fraternity there
were the Bullingdon Club, the Oxford Drag and the college point-to-points, called

Waldorf Astor at the head of the table at a dinner given by him after a day with the Oxford Draghounds.

'grinds.' If a young man who hunted went into the army the cavalry was his destination. 'We must put the boy in a good regiment,' the parents said, and the hunting son joined the Blues or the Hussars. Once there, apart from the odd piece of ceremonial duty there was nothing to prevent him from doing the society season as normal. And as for leave for hunting, there was never any doubt about that. With its test of courage and initiative it was, after all, preparation for warfare.

By around 1910 the agricultural depression had eased. A slow recovery had begun in the middle of the 1890s and with it a change in agriculture's chief produce. Milk had replaced wheat as the commodity in demand and to the contentment of the foxhunter many acres of grass remained pasture. The luxury identified with the reign of King Edward VII was at its zenith and it seemed there could be no turning back. Everywhere the country houses were being extended with fresh wings for more servants, more gardeners, more grooms and more stable-hands. The immortality of the Empire had been proclaimed at the Jubilee of the late Queen and any ripple on the surface of so solid a structure would surely disappear of its own accord.

There *was*, however, a ripple — a Liberal Government in power. And the new demon of the landed class was its Chancellor of the Exchequer, David Lloyd George. He was making inflammatory public speeches against private wealth and in favour of increased taxation. He was an aggressive teetotaller and he had motioned a

Waldorf Astor coming over the 25th fence to win the New College Grind in 1902.
Leaning back while jumping was a fashion quite common on the Continent at the time.

Licensing Bill threatening a reduction of public houses. At this point, Sir Gilbert Greenall tendered his resignation of the Belvoir, but the Lords rejected the Bill and Greenall continued. Only with its rejection did the absolute veto of the Lords begin to be in question. Next they sent back Lloyd George's 'People's Budget' — a budget devised to weaken the rich and undermine the hereditary principle. This was to be the campaign of the Ditchers, or Diehards, refusing the creation of 500 new peers. But the Lords finally capitulated in the face of Mr Asquith's Parliament Bill, and many of the intentions of David Lloyd George now became law.

But spirits continued high in the countryside. 'I'd rather be an M.F.H. than an M.P.', was the Jorrocks quote of the hunting men. The behaviour of Westminster did not register too deeply with them. All were agreed that it was enough to have

The confidence of hunting people shortly before the Great War. On the right is Victoria, Countess of Yarborough, visiting the Belvoir from her own pack, the Brocklesby. The Brocklesby had been run and owned by the Yarboroughs since the middle of the eighteenth century.

Riders in the Pytchley point-to-point of 1911. It was the custom to race in formal hunting dress.

men like Henry Chaplin fighting their cause. Chaplin's massive eighteen-stone bulk had become a respected sight on the Opposition benches. Descended from a long line of Lincolnshire squires, a landowner, hound-breeder and Master of Foxhounds, the counties of the kingdom could have no better representative. He knew about the laws and customs of the countryside and he was determined not to see that stability infringed. He had been appointed to the Royal Commission to inquire into the causes of the depression, and he made lengthy and researched speeches to explain the agricultural position. Concluding such a speech one day, Henry Chaplin turned to his friend and leader, Arthur Balfour. 'How did I do Arthur?' 'Splendidly, Harry, splendidly.' 'Did you understand me, Arthur?' 'Not a word, Harry, not a word.' In the cynical reply of Prime Minister Balfour, came a hint of the widespread confusion so soon to follow.

3

Bred for the Front

Cub-hunting was about to begin in England when war was declared on 4 August 1914. Since the assassination of the Archduke Ferdinand at Sarajevo in June, war had gradually seemed inevitable. None the less, few accepted the reality until Sir Edward Grey sent his ultimatum to Germany and even then it was thought the dispute would be settled in a matter of months. For the hunting men it was going to be sad indeed to miss the opening of a new season but here at last was their opportunity to show that courage prepared in the field. 'They shall do and they shall dare, as becomes their blood and their breeding,' wrote the editor of *Baily's*.

At the call for volunteers, men, boys and horses came forward from every hunting area in the kingdom. The horses were vitally required by the War Office from the first instance and within ten days of the declaration 15,000 hunters were ready for immediate departure. They were to make up half the cavalry contingent of the British Expeditionary Force. There was a sudden emptiness in the countryside as farmers' sons, tradesmen, hunt servants, labourers and sons of the county either enlisted to France or went into training with the yeomanry. The hunting fields were near-deserted with boys of twelve whipping-in and those Masters who remained riding ponies. All lawn meets were cancelled and no one wore scarlet. The largest field seen out during the 1914–15 season numbered twenty, including the hunt servants and the Master.

In the early days, it was believed that this would be a war fought on horse and the ancient yeomanry regiments were in expectation just as much as the smart cavalry regiments of Knightsbridge and Windsor. The yeomanry, after all, had a local distinction that was quite their own. Their origins stretched back to the sixteenth century when volunteer bodies had first coherently formed to defend the country against possible invasion from Spain. They had grown into their recognisable shape in the eighteenth century with fears of an invasion from France. Each county had its militia which fell under the jurisdiction of the Lord Lieutenant and was officered by the county families. Latterly the militia had come to be governed by the Army with the Lord Lieutenant acting as figurehead, but its conscription and organisation came from the county. Farmers and county tradespeople comprised its ranks while its officers were the sons, and often heirs, of the landed families. Every summer the yeomanry gathered for its annual camp when there were horse shows, ceremonials and happy, tipsy socialising. Nearly all the yeomanry hunted

The 2nd Life Guards leaving Windsor for the Front, 15 August 1914. At the head of the company is Captain Adrian Bethell, a foxhunting Yorkshire squire, and on his right a close friend, Sir Archibald Sinclair.

The Hertfordshire Yeomanry. At the head of the troop is the Hon. Thurstan Holland-Hibbert. The Yeomanry regiments were comprised mainly of farmers who brought their own horses to the front.

Holland-Hibbert's yeomanry troop in their stable clothes at the annual summer camp.

and the aspiration of every regular army adjutant sent to command a yeomanry force was a posting to a good hunting country.

And at the outset it was difficult for the young men to accustom themselves to the rigours of wartime. They had grown up in a period of prosperity and peace and found it hard to suppress their easygoing disposition. One young man, an habitué of the social calendar, when asked why he had not requisitioned any horses as instructed, replied that he was most terribly sorry but he was always in Scotland during August. Another, an officer in the Staffordshire Yeomanry, was sent by his commanding officer to buy six Shire horses suitable for pulling regimental stores. 'Go to the Potteries,' his commanding officer had advised. The young officer found five Shires but then a perfect hunter-type thoroughbred caught his eye and he could not resist. Writing up his report, he said about the sixth, 'This may not at first sight be exactly what's wanted, but he's sure to win a good heavyweight point-to-point!'

It was an unbearable wrench for 'the pick of our young fellows' not to be standing at covert-side, expectant of a fine run as hounds gave tongue. Year after year there had been that certainty and now their landscape was a blitzed terrain and their lodging a shelled estaminet. After the war, Siegfried Sassoon was to evoke that mood of the trenches in his semi-autobiographical *Memoirs of a Foxhunting Man*. He described his own fantasy, one shared by many:

> But even then it wasn't easy to think of dying . . . Still less so when Dick was with me, and we were having an imitation hunt. I used to pretend to be hunting a pack of hounds, with him as my whipper-in. Assuming a Denis Milden manner (Denis was at Rouen with the cavalry and likely to remain there, in spite of the C.O.'s assumptions about open warfare) I would go solemnly through a wood, cheering imaginary hounds. After an imaginary fox had been found, away we'd scuttle, looking in vain for a fence to jump, making imaginary casts after an imaginary check, and losing our fox when the horses had done enough galloping.

There was also Sassoon's boyhood friend from Kent, Stephen Colwood, who had sent in his subscription to the home pack. 'He must have sent it early in September, just before he was killed. No doubt he wrote the cheque in a daydream about hunting.' But for some the dream did come true. Thurstan Holland-Hibbert, who as Lord Knutsford was to become a well-known M.F.H. and amateur huntsman, managed to acquire several couple of hounds whilst behind the front line. As Holland-Hibbert and a handful of fellow-soldiers waited to go up the line, they occupied those listless days with hunting. The same courtesies of the chase were observed as in England. Permission was asked from the owners of nearby chateaux to draw coverts and the French clearly enjoyed the sight of these English officers realising their dreams. Not only was permission granted but in one chateau a hunt ball was arranged.

Meanwhile in London, the Masters of Foxhounds Association discussed how hunting should be carried on in the crisis. 'The great thing is not to let any hunt cease to exist,' said the Duke of Beaufort from the chair. There were strong reasons for this. A pack of hounds might be reduced in number but to lose a whole pack would involve years of re-grafting. Without regular hunting, the fox population would not be stabilised, and it was the hunt's duty to do this. Poultry-owners were

Cavalry officers hunting behind the lines while waiting for action. The hounds were acquired from the Crécy Boarhounds. Left to right: Lieut. Joe Dudgeon, Lieut. the Hon. Thurstan Holland-Hibbert, and Lieut. 'R. G.' Knowles.

All Right.

CHARLES LEJEUNE DE SCHIERVEL

CHATEAU DE MIELEN
(par Saint-Trond)

A card sent back from a château giving permission for the coverts to be drawn.

entitled to claim against the hunt if foxes killed their stock. However, economies were to be made. Couples of hounds would be reduced, second horses abandoned and the days per week of hunting cut back in most packs from four to two. Farmers rallied valiantly to aid the sport they loved. They agreed to take down wire at their own expense and often claims for damages were not presented.

For those above fighting age there were other uses too, besides guarding the pack. Throughout the country were the Remount Depots, taking in the new drafts of horses before their dispatch to the front. The sporting artist, Cecil Aldin, combined a Mastership of the South Berkshire with supervising a group of Remount Depots. At the outset there were still enough trained stablemen to look after the horses, which could number up to 300 at any one depot. But as the demand for more men at the Front increased, it became impossible to recruit professionals. One day Aldin found a man trembling with fear behind the horses. He announced that he was a tailor's cutter by trade and had never been near a horse before! Eventually, a tradition was broken, and women were called in.

The war, in general, brought out the talents of the hunting artists. Cecil Aldin painted scenes in the Remount Depot, Alfred Munnings was chosen to go to France to record the Canadian Cavalry Brigade, and Gilbert Holiday, one of the most gifted if, now, least known artists, made his way to the front before official war artists had been appointed and sent back unforgettable pictures of the action there. Lionel Edwards and G. D. Armour both worked and drew in the Remounts, but it was 'Snaffles' who was to touch the strongest chord in the hearts of hunting men.

'Snaffles' was the pseudonym of Charlie Johnson Payne. How or why Payne settled for a pseudonym is not related, except that it was entirely suitable. His paintings were more in the style of cartoons and although he lacked the technical accomplishments of Munnings, Edwards or Holiday, his work had an original feeling for situations. Snaffles had executed a series of cartoons on the hazards of the chase, but when war broke he went to France to illustrate life at the front for the *Graphic*. Among his drawings of soldiers crawling wounded through barbed wire, came several which referred to hunting. In an effort to sustain spirits, he would sometimes make light of the dreadful carnage with a metaphor about hunting the fox. But it was his print captioned 'That Far, Far Away Echo' which was to symbolise for thousands a universe that had slipped away. A soldier stands in his trench surrounded by a darkened, shelled landscape which is his nightmare, while in a corner is his dream: a huntsman cheers his hounds on, and a fox runs, just as it once was.

And indeed, at home, the hunting did survive in spite of severe difficulties. Although Canada was now contributing a large supply of horses to the front, the Army Council was continuing to draw heavily on the hunting establishments. The food shortage for both hounds and horses increased, and with conscription and an extended age limit, there was hardly a man left. Hunting the outlying areas of a 'country' had to cease through lack of rail transport and no petrol. With the season of 1917–18 the sport dropped to its lowest ebb, a result of the steady accumulation of difficulties. During a three-week frost even the Quorn hounds were turned out into the woods while the men stood ready with their guns. But such a measure would surely never be taken? When the soldiers came home on leave they must somehow find the hunting still there. It was this unswerving principle that made the cry of 'Carry on, Carry on' from the Masters of Foxhounds ever more determined.

For the first time, women came to the fore in the management of packs. Previously, there had been some who hunted packs of harriers, but to take charge of foxhounds was to make history. In several cases wives merely acted for their husbands at the front, but in others they assumed the full Mastership. A perfect instance was Mrs Inge with the well-known Midlands pack, the Atherstone. Her father had been Master and she lived on a handsome estate in the centre of the country. It was to the Atherstone that Siegfried Sassoon came in the season before war broke. He had gone from Kent to the Midlands on the encouragement of his friend, Norman Loder, who was to be Master for that season. In Sassoon's *Memoirs of a Foxhunting Man*, it is Loder who is described in the character of Denis Milden, the Atherstone is the Packlestone, and with Mrs Oakfield of Thurrow Park he gave an accurate account of Mrs Inge's popularity. It leaves no doubt as to her being the ideal choice for Master:

> An explanation of the continued prosperity of the Packlestone was
> largely to be found in Mrs Oakfield of Thurrow Park, a lady who
> made friends wherever she went. Since her childhood she had been
> intimately associated with the Hunt, for her father had been Master
> for more than twenty years. From her well-managed estate she set an
> example of up-to-date (though somewhat expensive) farm-manage-

Mrs Inge of Thorpe Hall in Staffordshire. With the men all at the Front, Mrs Inge accepted the invitation to become Master of the Atherstone in 1914. She was one of the first women to be a Master of Foxhounds. Siegfried Sassoon wrote her into Memoirs of a Foxhunting Man, *and referred to her as 'a lady who made friends wherever she went'.*

ment, and every farmer in the country (except a few stubborn Radicals) swore by Mrs Oakfield as the feminine gender of a jolly good fellow . . . The Packlestone farmers were proud to see Mrs Oakfield riding over their land – as well they might be, for it was a sight worth going a long way to see. A fine figure of a woman she was, they all agreed, as she sailed over the fences in her tall hat and perfectly fitting black habit with a bunch of violets in her button-hole. This brilliant horsewoman rode over the country in an apparently effortless manner . . . I admired Mrs Oakfield enormously; her quickness to hounds was a revelation to me, and in addition she was gracious and charming in manner. Whether she bowed her acknowledgment to a lifted hat at the meet or cantered easily at an awkward bit of timber in an otherwise unjumpable hedge, she possessed the secret of style.

From the front the men sent in their subscriptions to the packs as in peacetime, to bolster finances badly affected by war. Many knew that they might not hunt again and many came to question the purpose of the cavalry in a war of machine-gun fire, barbed wire and trenches. The yeomanry and cavalry regiments had gone out believing that they would charge and rout the enemy with their sabres bared. Such had been the belief of Haig, too. But it was the dug-out that the regiments experienced more than the mounted charge. By 1916 a large portion of the cavalry had become what was called 'mounted infantry' – a euphemistic term which did little to soften the blow. Those who were not now dismounted remained behind the lines with their horses, and it was a cavalry that was to see scant action before the German retreat of 1918. And yet a constant supply of horses was still necessary for pulling gun carriages, moving equipment and for the campaign in the desert. General Allenby's desert war was the last hope for the hunting man; the Western Front had proved to be muddle and bitter disappointment.

As the sporting men from Britain's counties died, *Baily's Directory* gave them their obituary, taking due note of the merit of each. 'Agar-Robartes, Hon. T.C., M.P., killed at the Front; hunted in Cornwall, played polo and knew a hunter.' 'Purser, Private ('Ginger') Jack (6th Batt. Y. and L. Regiment), well known to every one in the Oakley country as terrier man and a real good chap at his work.' 'Wyndham, Captain the Hon. W. R., a most enthusiastic foxhunter, throwing in his lot with the Belvoir.' 'Cleminson, Trooper Matthew, one of the gallant band of riding farmers in the York and Ainsty country.' 'Manners, Colonel Lord Robert, D.S.O. (Northumberland Fusiliers), an exceedingly cheery soul with all the Manners'

A rest period for the Scots Greys before the final advance across Northern France in 1918.

charm, and a great hunting man, putting in his six days a week in the happy old days.'

The language of *Baily's* was the currency of hunting people. It spoke their values and testified to the camaraderie which unites all who hunt. Throughout the Great War, *Baily's* viewed the catastrophe from the eyes of that diverse yet compact community. With a buoyant prose, it kept their spirits from flagging and made them know that their world — so small if set against larger events — had a purpose and would not be shattered. As the war dragged on, each issue contained a commentary on the state of battle. In words of sporting purple the battlefields became a foxhunt:

> True to our traditions, we are keeping the seas; and on land we are tenaciously following the selected line with increasing power and pace, and although the end of 'The Day' is not yet, the running is strong, the Hunt fresh, and the second horsemen are ready in reserve. Going to ground has not availed the quarry, for our 'Terriers' have bolted him in true sportsmanlike fashion and although he may run for many a mile, his heart is broken, he is well-nigh beat, and the hounds are close to his brush.

But *Baily's* metaphor was not out of place, for the men themselves sustained their morale by treating the exercise as a hunt. Dug-outs would bear the names of coverts, and over one was written 'Masters of Foxhounds Association.' There was

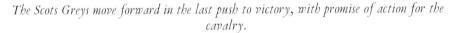

The Scots Greys move forward in the last push to victory, with promise of action for the cavalry.

an officer who led his yeomanry forward on the hunting horn. Across the crash of shells came the horn's rally of 'For'ard-away!' It was the hunting men's way of making light of the tragedy, their version of the stiff upper-lip implicit in their upbringing. They would rise above the deception of a war not made for cavalry and endure the agonies of machine-gun and rifle fire which ripped into their horses.

Some chargers were to survive the whole four and a quarter years of war. Understandably, their officers developed a strong attachment to them and when the war ended they brought them home. Many hunted again or even raced. General 'Jack' Seely's horse, Warrior, carried him through most of the grim cavalry action and went on to win a point-to-point after war's end. Seely wrote the story of his charger and recorded the effect of modern warfare on his horse. His description begs the question of the suitability of horses for warfare anyway:

> He must have hated the roar, but he thought it was all part of the curious game that he was playing, in which he had to learn to endure everything most hateful to him. For, see already to what he had been exposed – violent noise, the bursting of great shells (this he had already learnt to bear although so hateful to his acute ear) and bright flashes at night, when the white light of bursting shells must have caused violent pain to such sensitive eyes as horses possess. Above all, there was the smell of blood terrifying to every horse. Many people do not realise how acute is his sense of smell, but most of them will have read of his terror when he smells blood.

Foxhunting was in its second week of the new season when the Armistice was signed on 11 November 1918. In London there was general rejoicing. The streets were packed and the King was unable to make himself heard from the balcony of Buckingham Palace. In the country, within a few weeks, the hunting fields began to fill again and within a few months the country houses which had been requisitioned as hospitals resumed their former existence. Those who returned were keen to forget a war where friends had died by the hour. There was a determination to laugh and an insistence that normal life be resumed as quickly as possible. Although hunting had 'come through', it would take time before the packs could be back at full strength and the horse shortage resolved. Over 450,000 horses had gone from the United Kingdom to the war, and nearly half of that number were hunters. Apart from the officers with their chargers, none returned. The Army considered the expense of bringing them home too great. They were abandoned on the battlefields, along with other débris.

4
Between the Wars: a dream preserved

That air of unreality identified with the 1920s did not leave the hunting world untouched. A younger generation was growing up that was more tolerant of luxuries like the motor car which its fathers had despised. In the aftermath of war the sons and daughters of the gentry wanted enjoyment, and their pleasures were often to be found in the town rather than in entertaining in the county. The unbending attitudes of the previous generation held no scope for amusement and to many country estates came the fast lifestyle of Mayfair.

The landed gentry and aristocracy who pursued this more sophisticated approach to country living were not always as rich as the lifestyle demanded, but they frequently ignored this unpalatable fact. The shock of the Great War had been such as to create a euphoria – anything could come next, and Indian Summer or not, the hunting young of the Twenties were not to be put down. They would enjoy the standards of their predecessors while ridding themselves of the ethics of Empire. The accent on manliness through sport ceased to predominate, and with reason: that ethic had been slaughtered in the mud of Flanders. Hunting now needed no moral back-up. It was fun, a social activity.

English society was – and is, to an extent – made up of different 'sets'. The hunting set and the racing set by nature overlapped, but there was little exchange between these two sporting circles and 'the arts'. To a sporting person an interest in the arts covered all seemingly intellectual activity. Leicestershire had been appalled when one of its intimates, Margot Tennant, had married the Home Secretary, Henry Asquith. It did not matter that Miss Tennant herself was a member of an intellectual coterie, 'The Souls', because in Leicestershire she hunted. But now she had married a classical scholar. In the 1920s, however this antipathy between sets grew less rigid. For instance, the daughters of Lord Beauchamp hunted regularly, and with their brothers, Lord Elmley and the Hon. Hugh Lygon, played host to the aesthetes from Oxford. Lord Beauchamp's Worcestershire home, Madresfield, represented a centre of the civilised outlook to exotics like Brian Howard or writers like Evelyn Waugh.

Three of Earl Beauchamp's daughters at a meet of the Ledbury in Gloucestershire. Left to right: Lady Mary, Lady Sibell, and Lady Dorothy Lygon. They were friends with many of the notable Oxford undergraduates of the Twenties, and especially Evelyn Waugh.

The Oxford of the Twenties was largely responsible for this reconciliation of opposite cultures. The uniting factor was that neither group were there to work. The essential was pleasure, and if you found it hunting with the Heythrop or mixing a White Lady and reading Walter Pater it didn't matter so long as it was 'amusing'. A figure among the sportsmen was Hugh Sidebottom who, on coming down, was to set up as a trainer at Newmarket. Sidebottom's recall of Oxford in the middle Twenties is not of his studies, which he skilfully neglected, but of hunting

John Verney, the 20th Baron Willoughby de Broke and his wife leave Warwickshire for abroad in their Rolls-Royce Phantom.

A meet of the Oxford University Draghounds outside the Bear Inn at Woodstock in 1926. Left to right: Philip Kindersley, William Anstruther-Grey, Christopher Sykes, William Acton, the Hon. William Astor (Master), Bryan Guinness, Ian Sinclair, Hugh Sidebottom (whipper-in), Esmond Warner, James Phillips, unknown, and Smith, the kennel huntsman.

A hunting morning at Cliveden, just after the end of the war. Left to right: Winkie Brooks with his cousin the Hon. William (Bill) Astor.

and riding in the college grinds. At Christ Church he had adjacent rooms to an examplar of the aesthetes, William Acton. When Sidebottom broke his collar-bone in a grind, Acton insisted that during his recuperation he avail himself of his rooms. Suddenly Sidebottom found himself transported from his own sparse furnishings to a stage-set of lavishness. He lay for days on a deep-cushioned sofa gazing at Florentine tables and hangings, as the younger of the Acton brothers handed him potent aperitifs.

The image handed down of the Bullingdon is of a club whose main pastime was to mock aesthetes – Boy Mulcaster and his group of rowdy Bullingdon cronies ducking the effete Anthony Blanche in *Brideshead Revisited*. But this was not common to all. To be sure, there was an element of 'Let's put mustard down the backs of the aesthetes' in one or two excessively hearty types; but in general, the outdoor fraternity enjoyed their mutual pact with the more artistic, of no exertion beyond indulgence. And there were some who indulged with a single-mindedness that was almost ascetic. Hugh 'Grubby' Grosvenor hardly left his rooms unless it was to hunt or ride in a race. His father, Lord Stalbridge, was then Master of the Fernie and this smart post contrasted oddly with a son who had the toughness of a professional jockey. Grubby did become a high-class amateur, winning the Cheltenham Gold Cup. He cared for nothing else. 'All abroad's awful,' he used to say of anywhere that was not England and the turf.

Qualification for the Bullingdon was based chiefly on conviviality and a love of hunting. In the summer, to replace the lack of hunting, the Bullingdon held an annual cricket match. Either they played the Athenaeum (a Cambridge equivalent of the Bullingdon) or the Household Brigade. To members of the Bullingdon, the cricket match was meant to provide an occasion for entertainment, or even farce, but not serious cricket. The Household Brigade viewed the event differently. One

The Hon. Hugh Grosvenor winning the Christ Church Grind in February 1926.
Hugh Sidebottom is in the check colours.

Bullingdon Club members, 1928. Viscount Herbert and Lord Claude Hamilton play at burlesque rather than cricket. For the Bullingdon, the annual cricket match against either Cambridge's Athenaeum or the Household Brigade, was not taken seriously.

Robin Mount, a sporting undergraduate, takes a gate. The dash and devilry of the hunting field appealed to some of the Oxford aesthetes like William Acton, who would go out with the Drag and even ride in the Grinds.

summer, a keen Guards officer had broken his leave to travel up from the West Country for what he believed was to be a game of fine and testing cricket. True to his regimental training, he arrived at the ground to the minute of the hour appointed, only to find that cricket had been abandoned, pony racing was in full swing, and the cricket pavilion in flames.

With every thought turned to sport, amusement or decorative idling, taking a

On the left, Mr William Selby Lowndes of Whaddon Hall and Master of the Whaddon Chase, talking to Leopold Rothschild. The Selby Lowndes family had been Masters of the Whaddon for 200 years until, in 1920, a Rothschild faction ousted Bill Selby Lowndes. It was one of the most dramatic hunting rows ever to occur.

degree was secondary. Evelyn Waugh remarked in his autobiography, *A Little Learning*, how most of his generation went down with very bad ones. Hugh Sidebottom was to stay only two years. He avoided his first year's exam by faking illness, but by his second year it was necessary to show some willing. Part of the exam was to draw a map of France and this he could not do: it was said that he knew no more than three towns — Maisons-Laffite, Chantilly and Cannes. So he failed and regretfully left the pleasure-ground. Comforting him, a friend said, 'I think you're absolutely right to leave now. You couldn't have stood another year. It would have been too much.'

Meanwhile, in the hard core of the hunting world an unprecedented tussle for territory had taken place. The family of Selby Lowndes had hunted the Whaddon Chase for 200 years. The Mastership had been handed down from eldest son to eldest son. The Selby Lowndes were ancient gentry and one of the largest land-owners in Buckinghamshire. Their seat was Whaddon Hall, where they kennelled the hounds and hunted them as virtually a private pack. In the days of agricultural prosperity the family had been rich but from the depression of the 1870s onwards their fortunes had begun a slow decline. Throughout the troubles, they had invariably been sympathetic to their tenants, and with no assets beyond land, this had not helped their position. At the outbreak of war, the current incumbent, William Selby Lowndes, went to the front leaving his wife to manage the estate and the pack. He returned to find Lord Dalmeny hunting 'his' country with a separate pack.

From the late nineteenth century there had been a steady invasion of Rothschilds into Buckinghamshire. Waddesdon, Ascott, Tring and, by Lord Rosebery's marriage to Hannah Rothschild, Mentmore were the Rothschild fortresses of power. At the start the Rothschilds' hunting was confined to the carted stag, with permission from Selby Lowndes and the Whaddon Hunt Committee to perform their glorified drag over Whaddon country. But with Selby Lowndes away at the front, Lord Rothschild and several peers on the Whaddon Committee decided to oust Selby Lowndes from the Mastership and install Lord Dalmeny. The thinking behind the move was that Selby Lowndes no longer had the money to hunt the country while Dalmeny was half a Rothschild, heir to Lord Rosebery, and rich. Dispute at once ensued and resounded in *The Times*.

For a while the two packs hunted simultaneously, with Selby Lowndes ignoring the invaders. On one occasion Selby Lowndes and Dalmeny found themselves hunting the same fox and acrimony was quick to follow. Abuse led to the Masters dismounting from their horses and striking each other with their whips. The Masters of Foxhounds Association was increasingly embarrassed by the poor press the row was giving to hunting and referred to 'the deplorable state of affairs in the Whaddon country'. Yet it had no right to intervene since neither side had sought its arbitration. So the confusion thickened and doggerel circulated. Selby Lowndes had not been well treated, but what was wanted was a settlement:

The carted stag being set loose for Lord Rothschild's staghounds at Waddesdon. The stag is not killed but carted up again at the end of the day. It was a form of sport the Rothschilds enjoyed before they took to foxhunting.

In this crisis, my advice is
Toss a sporting penny.
Heads the hounds to Selby Lowndes
And tails to Lord Dalmeny.

Finally the dispute was brought to the Masters of Foxhounds Association. Both parties agreed to be bound by their decision and at a special meeting of the M.F.H.A. in December 1920 it was ruled that Selby Lowndes and Dalmeny should retire and the Whaddon Hunt Committee should hold a General Meeting to appoint a new Master. The Master elected was Lord Orkney, a peer in the Rothschild faction, and the choice appears to have been no more than a front, for within two seasons Dalmeny was back as Master. It was an instance of the ruthlessness of certain *nouveaux riches* to have what they wanted, no matter the means. The brusque handling of Selby Lowndes by Lord Dalmeny and his kinsmen could hardly have been more alien to the standards imbibed at Whaddon Hall.

The pattern of county life was clearly changing. Apart from a few brief periods of respite, agriculture had not regained its once prosperous footing. The progress made at the turn of the century had been largely cancelled out by the Great War, and there were many now like Selby Lowndes who either had to sell up or watch the gradual shrinkage of their estates. Rich townsmen were increasingly buying land from the fallen gentry. 'The last hour of the aristocracy has been sounded,' wrote Lord Ribblesdale, quoting Chateaubriand. It was discomfiting to the former Master of the Royal Buckhounds to observe this social upheaval, whatever the natural melancholy in his character. And yet those coming in without any rural background were keen to imitate the old order. Evelyn Waugh, for instance, was quick to spot the necessity of hunting. For some time he took serious tuition in equitation, so as to hold his own at Madresfield. But later he was to say of hunting, 'I didn't enjoy it', adding that he had done it 'only for social reasons.'

However the Selby Lowndes situation was not universal. There were still plenty of establishments, of sufficient size and resources, capable of taking a considerable economic buffeting before going under. In fact, a glance down the Court Circular columns of *The Times* for any day in the 1920s and 1930s would suggest that the British upper class was as flourishing as ever. It was the custom then to list one's every movement in the column: 'The Dowager Countess Cawdor and Lady Janet Gore have joined the house party at Cawdor Castle'; 'Lady Ludlow arrived at 82 Piccadilly yesterday from Newmarket'; 'The Marchioness of Carisbrooke is much better and has left for the country'; 'The Countess of Granard, with Lady Moira, Lady Eileen, and the Hon. John Forbes, will arrive at Southampton tomorrow in the Leviathan'; and so on day after day, year after year.

Movement was the keynote to the decades and when the crash of 1929 happened it did not cease. The country-house parties for the fashionable race meetings were reported in *The Times*, along with detailed accounts of the ladies' dresses. If one stayed in a hunting house in the winter – and most did – one was expected to hunt. The next night one might be dancing at the Embassy, Quaglino's or the Café de Paris, returning the following day to the the country to stay somewhere else. 'The weekend' visit was popular, but, for a class not yet familiar with 'the office', visits could be constant and last from a few days to a few weeks. Aldous Huxley caught the atmosphere in *Crome Yellow*, his satire of the Twenties:

> Ivor was gone. Lounging behind the windscreen in his yellow sedan he was whirling across rural England. Social and amorous engagements of the most urgent character called him from hall to baronial hall, from castle to castle, from Elizabethan manor-house to Georgian mansion, over the whole expanse of the kingdom. Today in Somerset, tomorrow in Warwickshire, on Saturday in the West Riding, by Tuesday morning in Argyll – Ivor never rested.

Lord Willoughby de Broke discussing the coverts to be drawn with his huntsman, Ted Cox, at a meet of the Warwickshire at Shuckburgh Park in 1934. Lord Willoughby de Broke continued the family tradition of being Master of the pack.

Hunting society on holiday in Biarritz, August 1935. Back row, left to right: Teddie Cook, Pat Adamson, Nancy Paget, Lord Willoughby de Broke. Front row, left to right: Reggie Paget, Jane Wright, Lady Willoughby de Broke, Kenneth Grant.

Although the cost of keeping a pack of hounds had risen by 250 per cent since 1914, hunting had fully recovered its former strength. An ever increasing supply of money from the new industrial and business class, now modestly landed, had helped. A Joint-Mastership was almost unheard of before 1914, but between the wars it was to become relatively frequent and accepted. One Master supplied the image of ancient nobility, the other supplied the cash. The landed gentry and aristocracy were not the less respected for bowing to this compromise. They remained the vital figureheads, without whom there would be no one for the recently arrived to imitate.

The effect on hunting of a more fluid society was apparent on the surface, but not as yet structural. The sons of country families were still taught to ride by the groom, and, in the expectation that they would be ardent foxhunters, were usually sent on to Eton where for early practice the College beagles awaited them. Two boys who went there during this time and showed signs of hunting promise through their Mastership of that school pack were Captain 'Ronnie' Wallace and Lord Hugh Percy (now the Duke of Northumberland). In an obituary notice of an earlier Master of the College Beagles, a hint of their importance is made clear. It should be no surprise that this Master was a Selby Lowndes: 'It may truly be said of the late Mr Lowndes that he came into the world to send foxes out of it, and, like many others since his day, he learnt the early lessons of his craft while carrying the horn with the Eton Beagles, where he was entered to hunt almost as early as to Horace and Virgil.'

In the late 1920s a storm broke which had been gathering force since the 1890s. It concerned the breeding of the recognised foxhound. A number of Masters had long believed that the blood in the approved breeding lines was thinning. The answer was an outcross and they turned to Wales. But in the minds of traditionalists this was an unthinkable step. Lord Willoughby de Broke, Master of the Warwickshire, and in charge of a 'governing' kennel breeding the pure English hound, had stated, 'It is a mistake to go too far away in blood. To take an extreme case, a fantastic alliance between an English foxhound and a Welsh foxhound, who have no ancestors in common, is calculated to produce a family of freaks of no recognised type.' Others

The Hon. Michael Willoughby hunting with the Middleton in the 1930s during his school holidays from Eton.

*Lord Hugh Percy (later the Duke of Northumberland), Master of the Eton Beagles,
hunting them from home at Alnwick Castle, Northumberland, in August 1931.*

did not agree, and perhaps it was fortunate for Lord Willoughby de Broke that he
did not live to see the full proliferation of the clotted-cream colouring of the Welsh
hound in sacred English kennels.

Lord Willoughby de Broke and foxhunters of his generation did not wish to face
the inevitability of changing circumstances. Apart from the weakening of stamina
through inbreeding, it was argued, the type of hound now needed to negotiate
tarmac roads, motor cars and deeper ploughing required a robustness of nose and
physique which the English foxhound did not possess. The English foxhound had
been bred for grass country, light plough and none of the distractions to scent that
the machine age was inducing. Speed he did have, and in particular the bitches;
in the flying Shires the bitches alone were used to hunt in the fastest country,
though it had been found that the Welsh hound had exceptional nose, stamina, and
'cry'.

However, a foxhunting oligarchy was determined to keep the Welsh blood out.
The prizes at Peterborough were awarded to the traditional foxhounds only. And
some of these hounds, the dissenters said, no longer stood straight, and appeared in
various respects misshapen. Among the voices of dissent was Isaac ('Ikey') Bell, an
American by birth who had been educated and brought up in England. Visiting the
hounds of Sir Edward Curre one day, a noted breeder who hunted a private pack
round Chepstow, Bell was impressed by the performance of Curre's hounds. They
were his first outcross of breeding from pure Welsh, and entered in the Stud Book
since Curre's was a recognised kennel. Bell, a Master himself, began to breed from
them and the idea spread. Soon a 'governing' kennel such as the Duke of Beaufort's
was breeding from them, and the Masters of Foxhounds Association decided that
they must act.

The Eton College Beagles in 1938. In the centre is Ronnie Wallace, Master of the Beagles, with his five whippers-in. The whippers-in from left to right are: Francis Collin, Mark Mainwaring, Michael de Chair, Jonathan Blow, and the Hon. Julian Holland-Hibbert. Next to Holland-Hibbert is Perkins, the kennel huntsman.

The Duke of Beaufort with his hounds at Badminton. The Duke was one who favoured the introduction of Welsh blood into these traditional English foxhounds.

The hunt servants at Badminton in the 1930s. Left to right: T. Reed (2nd Whipper-in), Tom Newman (huntsman), George Castle (1st Whipper-in).

At a meeting chaired by Lord Bathurst, the rule for a hound's admittance to the Kennel Stud Book was altered. Every hound had now to 'have been bred, entered and worked in a recognised foxhound kennel, besides which their sires and dams, or both their grand-sires and both their grand-dams must have been registered in the Foxhound Kennel Stud Book.' The alteration made it no longer possible for the hound and its sire and dam simply to be bred and worked in a recognised kennel for entry, and thus any further intrusion of Welsh blood was prevented. But the ruling could not eradicate the blood already there, and so crossing back the breeding went on.

Those who favoured the English foxhound were not at all pleased that this intrusion could go on. A few years later the storm broke again. On Ikey Bell's retirement as Master of the South and West Wilts, the hunting correspondent of *The Times* published an eulogistic piece, praising his foresight and imagination. He accused the antagonists of sitting back in their armchairs and dreaming of pre-war splendours. The English foxhound, he reckoned had grown, 'as slow as the Durham Ox.' Surely it was a relief when 'the door opened to admit a draught of fresh air and Mr Isaac

Bell'. The response was swift. Robert Brassey, son of Albert, wrote to *The Times* with indignation. 'Where would it end?' he demanded. The hunting correspondent stuck to his opinions. Brassey returned in kind, and this time the hunting correspondent replied, a little more curtly: 'I can breed good stallion hounds from an armchair just as well as you can.' But Brassey had his supporters. Lord Bathurst wrote privately to him: 'I agree with you that he (Bell) has done no end of harm to the English foxhound. Now that he has retired I hope this propaganda will cease and that in time they will breed out the Welsh – the little sharp bitches that he likes will cure themselves by breeding rats.' From Sussex came consolation from another distinguished hunting peer, Lord Leconfield at Petworth: 'I am not surprised at the answer of the Hunting Editor of *The Times* because that journal is very much inclined to only print its own view. Does it matter much what it says?'

Yet time and experience were to show whether the argument for Welsh blood was as fully convincing as the protagonists made out. There were packs who wanted none of it, claiming that the Welsh foxhound was too individual and, being basically a hill hound, was slower than the English foxhound. The Shire packs, especially, remained keen to avoid the strain. Across the light Shire grassland the English hounds were ideal, hunting close together and with the turn-of-foot vital to the terrain. But the debate for and against continued, consuming the writing paper and

Lord Leconfield, Master of his own hounds from 1901 to 1942, making a speech from the steps of his home, Petworth House, in Sussex. Lord Leconfield was among those who did not approve of introducing the Welsh strain into the English hound. Standing behind him is Lady Leconfield.

after-dinner hours of Masters and huntsmen alike.

It was after the Great War that Siegfried Sassoon wrote his testament to the hunting idyll of his youth. He had lived for that circumscribed world of country people with their innocence and their unity, but the war had shattered his own innocence and he hardly returned to it. Since his long discussions into the night with his hunting mentor, Norman Loder, he had become a celebrated war poet and he now had friends in circles where hunting did not signify. He could not mix the two worlds and he felt acute embarrassment when Norman Loder called on him at the house of his new artistic friends, the Sitwells. Loder could not make out the strange modern paintings on the walls and asked Sassoon in a hushed undertone, 'Who *are* these Sitwells?' Unlike the Oxford undergraduates, Sassoon felt guilty about his association with these simple friends who would be judged Philistines by the intellectual drawing-rooms where he had found favour.

Occasionally Sassoon hunted or rode in a point-to-point but it was not with the same ease as before. He had spoken in his *Memoirs of a Foxhunting Man* of his loss of conviction when he came home on leave and stared round the room at the photographs of his hunters. The year 1914 had made that the past for him. His fame as a poet had partly replaced his early enthusiasm, except that when he wrote of hunting or of racing in his journals and diaries he treated it as a romance stifled. Caring for his artistic reputation, he could not reconcile himself to these activities, and in his struggle to suppress them he was to add to the melancholy and introspection which eventually overcame him.

Siegfried Sassoon was not the only writer to hunt and try to rationalise it. In the 1930s the novelist, T. H. White, having taught at Stowe School for four years, then took a cottage in the woods and grassy avenues known as Stowe Ridings. It was there that White attempted to train the falcon which resulted in *The Goshawk*. At Stowe, White had taken to hunting and went out frequently with the Grafton. He was to be seen coming out of school on a Saturday morning, hurriedly tearing off his grey flannel trousers to reveal breeches and boots, and dashing away in his car to join the hunt.

For T. H. White hunting was getting to know the countryside and what happened in it. He had no time for those who see the country as a landscape waiting to be tamed by the genteel creeds of urban humanitarians. Living amongst nature meant hunting, fishing and shooting – and White did all three. He kept a journal for each which he afterwards published as the book *England Have My Bones*. About hunting White was a realist. On the romantic side, he did not mind dull days when he could stare at nature. Otherwise, he did not believe that, by hunting foxes, 'slaughter coarsens the soul'. He admired the skill of the hunter and the hunted, and he thought it false to equate animal with human suffering. As to other methods of killing the fox he was against shooting. He had once tried – in a non-hunting country, he quickly adds – and the result was miserable. No, White concludes,

I should prefer to be hunted; rather than to be left to rot with gangrene, or to gnaw my paw off in a steel trap, or to fear all food in case it should contain that fatal dusting of strychnine which would kill me in a writhing agony, curling my backbone till my mask touched my brush. If it comes to that I should always prefer to die fighting (the hounds kill a fox in a second) and shall make a point of trying to knock down my gaolers when they come to hang me for poisoning my future wife.

During his years at Stowe, White came to understand about farming, the countryside, and the life out-of-doors. What he feared was a society losing touch with place. The countryside was not lived in as it once had been and people had grown dependent on an artificial world 'where water is an idea that comes out of a tap, and light a conception in a switch'. How to stop the flood of ignorance engendered by cities and the make-believe rusticity of the garden suburbs? 'I am an *Englishman*, and I live in the *shire*,' was T. H. White's attitude, and he spoke his mind. He recommended for his urban communist friends 'a toss over timber' and complained that they had lost their centre of gravity. 'They lean against the mantelpiece at the wrong angle, and the fender slips, and bang goes one of the candlesticks — broken.' A spell out-of-doors, he preached, learning again to grapple with the basics, would restore the balance of their minds and bodies.

The dream of T. H. White was to preserve the countryside and all its healthy customs against invasion and rule by the town-dweller with his lost identity. He had a hideous vision of a likely future, which now has been far surpassed. It was the prettiest counties which would be their immediate prey, and go first. Sussex and Devon, White said, had already gone and next, 'The invaders will top the skyline, marching under petrol pumps and curiosity shops and corrugated iron roofs. Gloucestershire, whose architecture grows out of the earth, because it builds with the stone it stands on, will blossom with red brick and blue slates. Wiltshire, whose downs enclose fertile valleys, will bloom with loop-ways and mustard-yellow touring signs and gentlemen from the A.A.'

But whatever the portents might be, the hunting world was not to be thwarted. Machines were replacing horses on farms, cars replacing the pony-trap, and everywhere a horse-oriented society seemed to be on the retreat. To safeguard an interest in the horse for future generations and to combat the advance of the machine, the Pony Club was founded. Its explicit purpose was the encouragement of children to ride and to understand about horses. Gymkhanas, children's meets and hunter trials began. Instructors toured the country teaching the same manners and discipline as were expected on the hunting field. Thousands had soon joined the Pony Club, each hunt had its branch, and all over the country there were scenes to be immortalised by Thelwell. And with it, the type of person who hunted broadened. The old

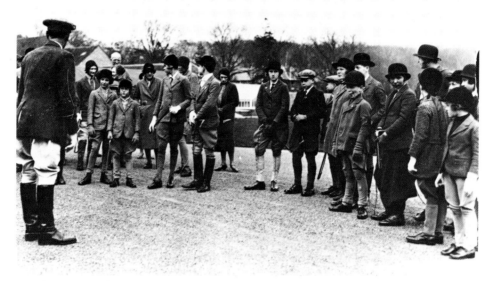

Belvoir Pony Club children being addressed during the early days of the Pony Club in the 1930s.

Ivry (left) and Janetta Paynter, the daughters of the well-known amateur rider George Paynter, at a Belvoir meet.

Lord Grimthorpe, Joint-Master of the Middleton, addressing children at a Pony Club meet at Birdsall in 1932.

The author's father, Purcell Blow, competing in the Berkeley hunter trials, 1936.

The Sinnington point-to-point, 1929. Left to right: Lord Feversham, Griselda Grant-Lawson, Phyllis Foster, and Victoria Worsley.

combination of landowner and farmer now had an infiltration of town tradespeople and local businessmen.

As the Masters were arguing over hound-breeding, the Wall Street crash of 1929 came. It echoed back to the London Stock Exchange and sent prices sliding, placing an instant restriction on credit. By 1930 England was in the grip of its Great Depression, bringing mass unemployment and, for the farmer, no outlets for his produce. Once again, wherever they could, landlords waived or reduced tenants' rents, but this was not enough. The consequences of this second agricultural depression were to be far greater than before. Farmers were going bankrupt, abandoning the land and filling the ranks of the unemployed. Some attempted to live by barter, shooting and selling rabbits and such like, but for most it meant the end of a life on the land. Between 1929 and 1933 over 2000 farmers went bankrupt. In Lincolnshire, Lord Yarborough took back 11,000 acres of deserted holdings. The value of land had fallen to nearly £10 an acre.

Spectators at the Fernie point-to-point. Left to right: Patsy Ward, Audrey Coats, Betty Grosvenor, and Mrs Brassey.

The Drummond family (of Drummond's Bank) at a Pytchley point-to-point in the 1930s.

The sight of derelict farms and land lying idle became commonplace. The Labour Government in office when the Depression began did little for the farmers, whereas support was given to other failing industries. The Government did not wish to to alleviate a situation which might also improve the finances of the land-owners. But the Government did not understand the close inter-dependence of relationships in the countryside. As urban sympathisers, they did not particularly care for what appeared an anachronistic environment. Never had the division be-tween town and country been so great.

For those farmers who were managing to survive, the hunting field became the centre of rural unity. Here, among their fellow-men, they found protection from a wider society that was largely indifferent to them. Here they could discuss their problems whilst enjoying the relaxation from tension. If the landowner or his agent were out, the difficulties of paying rent or wasting crops would be spoken of directly, without embarrassment. Adrian Scrope, then agent for his brother-in-law, Sir Richard Sykes, at Sledmere, dealt with most of the tenants' problems while out hunting. Usually a bank was threatening to foreclose, and sometimes Scrope would

Farmers and landowners show their united front in the Depression. With these Yorkshire farmers are Bernard, Duke of Norfolk (fourth from left) and Adrian Scrope (sixth from left), agent to his brother-in-law Sir Richard Sykes at Sledmere.

The kind of countryman that hunting people depend on. T. R. Davies, a great support to Lord Knutsford (then Thurstan Holland-Hibbert) when he was hunting the Teme Valley pack in Wales.

A respected figure with every hunt. Webb, the terrier man, at Badminton. Terriers are used to bolt the fox when he has gone to ground.

A presentation to Ronald Tree at Kelmarsh Hall in 1933 on his retirement as Joint-Master of the Pytchley for seven years. Left to right: Mrs (Nancy) Tree, Sir Charles Frederick, Ronald Tree, and the Hon Mrs Jack Lowther.

Hunting army officers make their way to the start at the Aldershot point-to-point in the 1930s. On the left is the Hon. Ronald Strutt (later Lord Belper).

give tenants £50 out of his own pocket to stave off disaster. Contrary to the popular concept of the brutish squire, the farming ranks drew together to defend their cause.

But it was not only the tenant farmers who were in debt with the bank; frequently the landlords were, too. Estates of 3000 acres or less had to be sold unless the owner had an income from business. It was the size of estate that the new rich were buying, yet it was the beginning of the end for the smaller squirearchy. However, the squirearchial estates of 6–10,000 acres usually did come through, although not easily. The need for bank loans was constant and yet it was this larger squirearchy and landed aristocracy who tended not to accept any change in lifestyle.

Baily's Directory recorded 'excellent' sport throughout the 1930s, and that hunting was so curiously unaffected by the Depression was in part due to the resolution of these gentlemen not to surrender. Their attitude might have been unrealistic, but it had charm and a lovable naivety. At Rise Park, in the East Riding of Yorkshire, Adrian Bethell was the very image of the foxhunting soldier-squire. A young officer in the Household Cavalry during the Great War, he had come back to his family estate to hunt. The Depression struck just as Bethell had taken over the Mastership of the Holderness Hunt. With his income halved, Bethell refused to reduce either his hunting or the scale of his living. In the house, which was a substantial mansion, he kept a butler and two footmen, and in the stables there were twenty horses with a man for every two. To live as he had always done, he persuaded the bank to grant him a large overdraft which was to be set against the

Hunting through the Depression at Badminton. Left to right: Lady Helena Gibbs, the Earl of Westmorland, the Duchess of Beaufort.

Captain Adrian Bethell of Rise Park in the East Riding of Yorkshire, with his daughter, Diana. Adrian Bethell was typical of the landowner who refused to compromise either his hunting or his style of living in the depressed 1930s.

Captain Tom Wickham-Boynton, hunting the Middleton East Hounds, attends the kill.

value of his near valueless acres. But to show the bank manager that he was holding his own, he gave the iron gates to the lodges at Rise a fresh coat of paint every year. As the bank manager drove past the lodges on his way to work each morning, he was sure to be impressed and have complete confidence that Captain Bethell was in control, if not making money.

Only the spending escalated. Soon the hounds were kennelled at Rise and Bethell was hunting them himself. Now dogs and kennellmen were added to an already large staff and there had to come a cut. Resourcefully, Adrian Bethell found a way out. His father, a widower for many years, had felt compelled to assemble an important collection of early pornographic books. These books would fetch something on the private market, and when a crisis was about to break — and they were not infrequent — he sold a few. Thus neither house, hunting nor hounds were sacrificed, and a friend writing to *The Times* on Adrian Bethell's death could safely say, 'He would not give up what he considered was his right — in fact, the right of every Englishman — his home.'

That *Times* obituary went on to speak of 'Adrian's excitement as he followed his hounds across that great drain country where he belonged.' For the Master to hunt his hounds himself was a legacy from the eighteenth century which had persisted. It dated back to that period when the squire hunted for the entertainment of his neighbours, and with families who had lived and hunted in the same area for generations there was a precedence of tradition. The list of landowner-huntsmen was headed by the Duke of Beaufort, who, until his recent retirement, hunted the Beaufort on a level with the professionals. But there were several, whether land-

Alan Orr-Ewing and Chum Ponsonby dressed as jockey pages for the wedding of George Paynter. They are wearing Colonel Paynter's National Hunt colours.

Miss Guest, daughter of Merthyr Guest, at a meet of her own pack at Wraxall in Somerset, 1932. She is talking to Mrs Neal, a hunting neighbour. Miss Guest had her own pack of hounds for nearly fifty years.

Miss Guest's hounds unloading at the meet.

owners or simply obsessed by foxhunting, who attained considerable excellence in the art. Some treated it with serious dedication, others were more light-hearted. Lord Feversham, Master and huntsman of the Sinnington, always found the specialised 'hound talk' difficult. When encouraging them on, he used to warble 'Greta Garbo, Greta Garbo.' It was the best he could manage. Once the hounds had grown used to this individual note, it worked.

But to see families like the Bethells hunting their hounds over land they had lived on for generations gave a continuing sense of security at a vital moment. For if the county structure were to vanish where could the farmer turn then? The landlord understood the plight of his tenants and the small independent farmer, and his aid was more forthcoming than that of the government official sent on a tour of inspection. By the middle of the 1930s attempts were made to rescue the farmers, but government subsidies were either inadequate or misdirected. The gap between theory and practice had grown so great that often they did more harm than good.

Nobody knew about the land any more, and the farmers wondered whether Whitehall really cared.

So if successive governments did not help the farmer, the landed gentry would. By fighting for their houses, their estates and their hunting, they preserved the backbone of country life. While they remained there could be employment for the

The Munich crisis draws closer but the hunting camaraderie goes on. A meet of the Percy at Westnewton House, Woller, Northumberland. Left to right: Lady Elizabeth Percy, Lady Diana Percy, their mother Helen, Duchess of Northumberland, and Captain the Hon. Claud Lambton.

Lord Feversham prepares for war with the Yorkshire Yeomanry.

labourer, and while hunting remained there was the need for hunters. For not a few farmers the breeding of hunters became the last source of reliable revenue. And this firm resolution of farmer and gentry to stand as one was to provide a rare corner of refuge in a decade of anxiety. Lord Halifax, who was obliged to spend most of that decade in a variety of political posts, eagerly looked forward to a return home whenever pressure relaxed. Back in Yorkshire, he could resume his hunting with the Middleton and talks with his tenants on his estate at Garrowby. Like Lord Spencer of an earlier age, Halifax found hunting and the company of country people a valued antidote to 'dull care'.

By the time of the Munich conference, it seemed inevitable that another catastrophe was imminent. But the countryside went on undeterred, held together by the calm of its own making. The large houses, with the communities dependent on them; the villages with their artisans; the pub with its mellow corner of local gossip; talk of the weather, the 'big' house, cricket, or yesterday's sport with the hounds – all continued in a countryside where inns still took in horses, the villages had not lost all their young to the cities, and not every road had been blackened by tarmac and exhaust. In the people themselves there was an individuality which had not been frightened out of them by despair. Across the Channel a Nazi Germany was preparing, but in the country there was still an element of a Shakespearian England.

5

High Style in the Shires

If you had stopped a while at Melton Mowbray in the 1920s you would not have believed that war had disrupted a national economy. Nor would you have imagined that hunting had been through a very grim period. That spirit of euphoria which had struck the affluent was nowhere more in evidence than in the flying grass countries of the Shires. But it was not just the brittle talk of Mayfair which was transported to hard-riding Leicestershire; around Melton there gathered a hunting set dedicated to giving the sport a flamboyance that would have startled even their luxury-conscious forebears. Their antecedents lay with the recklessness of the Regency. The Twenties, we know, was a carefree age for many, and for proof of that in sporting circles, it was necessary to go no further than Melton.

The hunting lodges of that town, already steeped with a certain rakish folklore, now blossomed in a new eminence. They became the winter playgrounds for those who needed to spend and to entertain with all the embellishments that their wealth could buy. The yard of every lodge abounded with horses and grooms while the houses were filled with aristocrats, bankers, royalty and bounders. Clover Clubs and White Ladies were the cocktails shaken at The Embassy Dance Club, modelled on its metropolitan namesake in London. From November to April the socialites of a fast and international Melton dined and danced as regularly as they hunted.

But in spite of the invasion, there were also those whose roots were in the county. The family of Major 'Algie' Burnaby had always lived at Baggrave Hall, an eighteenth-century squire's seat, and it had long been used for hunting. Burnaby's fame dated back to the 1890s when he had won the Moonlight Steeplechase. It was an idea of the moment and all the participants had ridden with night-shirts over their scarlet coats and breeches. But Burnaby had forgotten his night-shirt and he had won the race in a pink, beribboned night-dress lent by Lady Augusta Fane. At Baggrave the spending was as quick as elsewhere. The accent was on poker, and, as becomes a gambling house, both house and estate were mortgaged. Algie Burnaby was a highly popular Master of the Quorn throughout the Twenties, and described

The opening meet of the Quorn at Kirby Gate in the middle Twenties. Left to right: Lady de Trafford, the Marchioness of Blandford, and Chinti de Paravacini.

The Quorn moving off from Kirby Gate. The fields could number almost 400. Fashionable Melton leads this field – riding behind the whipper-in is Charlie Carlos-Clarke who composed doggerel rhymes on the socialites.

Dressing up was a regular highlight. Fancy-dress revellers group themselves down the staircase at Melton's renowned Craven Lodge, February 1923.

Two fashionable visitors to Melton. The Countess of Dalkeith and the Earl of Carnarvon.

*Phyllis Cantrell-Hubbersty with John Nutting (a son of Sir Harold Nutting) and,
far right, a hunting friend at a meet of the Quorn in the 1930s.*

Major Algie Burnaby, Master of the Quorn in the Twenties, gives a talk at a children's meet from the steps of his home, Baggrave Hall.

as 'a charmer'. He had a reputation as a womaniser which sometimes earned him the dubbing of 'a rogue'. His first wife, pining for a more artistic milieu, had left him. But Burnaby soon replaced her with a rich American lady, and so the gambling and the hunting went on.

It was a world waiting for the pen of William Makepeace Thackeray rather than R. S. Surtees; for Melton's similarities lay with *Vanity Fair* rather than Jorrocks, and there was no shortage of men like Sir Rawdon Crawley and women like Becky Sharp. In the mould of Sir Rawdon Crawley was the Honourable Lionel Tennyson, one of the earliest arrivals at Melton after the Great War. Tennyson had run off with the wife of Adrian Bethell and was now married to her. His wife, Clare, was celebrated for her beauty and had a following of admirers as numerous as Diana Cooper's. Tennyson's reputation was for cricket, and on several occasions he was captain of England. But his notoriety was for drinking and spending. He hunted, but not seriously, and he had come to Melton explicitly for the pleasures available. He was not well-off, having already spent a fair portion of an inheritance earned painstakingly by his grandfather the poet. But his wife had money, and others entertained him. Lionel was proud of his grandfather, Alfred, but sad that the

Lady Eileen Clarke (wife of Charlie Carlos-Clarke) and the Hon. Lionel Tennyson at Craven Lodge in 1923.

mantle of poetic ability had not fallen on his own shoulders. Unable to pronounce his 'r's', he would be heard to matter, 'I could have wwitten all that, if only I could have thought of the wuddy whyme.'

Aristocracy and squires mixed with businessmen, entrepreneurs and tycoons. The fortune of Mr Ambrose Clarke came from Singer sewing machines and at Warwick Lodge he stabled fifty thoroughbred hunters – double in number to most yards. Melton also had a resident financial adviser – the millionaire, Mr Lowenstein, called 'Low' by his friends, who kept a yard of magnificent horses in the nearby village of Thorpe Satchville, and gave investment advice on the hunting field. One day a client was furious because the shares had not risen as expected, and he went for 'Low' with his crop. Immediately afterwards the shares rose, but the client had already sold. Later poor Mr Lowenstein was to have a tragic end. He fell out of his private aeroplane while crossing the Channel; no one knew if it was an accident or if he had been pushed.

The Hon. Mrs Lionel Tennyson, a celebrated society beauty, with her friend, Miss Monica Sheriffe.

*The Earl of Westmorland ('Burghie') was a frequent visitor to the Shires. Unlike other
Meltonians, he had not much money, but he would ride whatever horse available.*

*Second left, Sir Harold Nutting, Master of the Quorn, with Major Philip Cantrell-
Hubbersty, judging the equitation test at the Quorn Pony Club Gymkhana in 1937.*

Four Cadogan daughters of Viscount Chelsea, who all married hunting men. Left to right: Lady Hillingdon (Edith), the Marchioness of Blandford (Mary), Lady de Trafford (Cynthia), and Lady Edward Stanley (Portia). The last three hunted regularly from Melton, Lady Hillingdon with the Grafton. The four husbands were jocularly referred to as 'Cadogan Square'.

The money now paying for hunting came chiefly from industrial or manufacturing sources. It had reached second or third generation, with heirs nicely distanced from the necessity to earn. To take three examples of rich Masters whose incomes were derived from these sources, there were George Colman of the Belvoir, 'mustard'; Sir Harold Nutting of the Quorn, 'bottling Guinness'; and Major 'Tommy' Bouch, also of the Belvoir, 'construction engineering'. On occasion the interest in the bank balance could be made quite plain. Sir Harold Nutting was to spare no expense when he financed the Quorn, but he was not known as a character that would keep Melton in laughter. Algie Burnaby, inviting Nutting to join him as Joint-Master, told him, 'We don't want your personality, we want your purse.' The two Masters were not to become friends.

When, in 1923, the Prince of Wales started to hunt from Melton, the keenness to be seen there grew more urgent. An ex-officer, Major-General Vaughan, had already turned Craven Lodge into a hunting guest-house with stabling for the guest's horses. You took either a room or a suite for the season, and it was here that the Prince of Wales installed himself. From the Royal suite he gave dinner parties and dinner dances, and ladies vied with each other to be included in his set. The local neighbourhood adored the Prince, who was an artist of 'the common touch', but closer friends did not always find him easy. He could be changeable; at one moment relaxed and speaking an affected cockney, and the next over-aware of his station.

Inevitably, Melton Mowbray had all the making of a snob's paradise. By the middle Twenties, it not only had a galaxy of titles but three Royal Princes hunting. Prince Henry and Prince George were also to be regulars, sharing the Royal suite. Practical jokes became a fashion, one of which was to ask those women known to be in pursuit of the Prince of Wales to an imaginary dinner party. The girl would desperately search for a flattering partner and then turn up on the steps of Craven Lodge to be told that the Prince was in London. A few men with foreign names decided it would help to add a title after a season. Mr Jack de Pret suddenly returned as Count de Pret, and alerted people's suspicions. To some, it was important to be seen hunting when the right people were out. Lady Ancaster (or Eloise to friends) was an American said to have Indian blood ('those high cheek-bones'), and coming

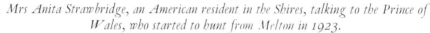

Mrs Anita Strawbridge, an American resident in the Shires, talking to the Prince of Wales, who started to hunt from Melton in 1923.

108

The Countess of Ancaster (Eloise) with the Cottesmore. She only liked to hunt on the fashionable days, and she is turning round here to make sure that the 'right' people are out.

The Hon. George Lambton, taking time off from his training establishment at Newmarket, and the Marchioness of Blandford.

from the Ancaster seat of Grimsthorpe, she was nearer the Cottesmore country. At meets she would look round anxiously and ask, lest she had made a mistake, 'Where are the Melton people?'

The three packs that 'the right people' hunted with from Melton were the Quorn, Belvoir and Cottesmore. Each had their fashionable days which were dictated by the quality of the country hunted over. Mondays and Fridays were the Quorn, Tuesday the Cottesmore, Wednesday the Belvoir, and Saturday the Belvoir or the Cottesmore. The Fernie, although also a Shire pack, was too far for most Meltonians, who anyway had these three prize packs on their doorstep. But the dedicated hard riders went there, making it their 'Thursday'. The general rule was to hunt four or five days in a week, except for the truly ardent sportsmen who might hunt six. If you were a fun-loving Meltonian, you were also always out in the evenings. Miss Monica Sheriffe, in the first flight of Meltonian sportswomen and party-goers, only spent one evening a fortnight at home.

The dinners and parties which awaited one after hunting were a further form of exercise in themselves. After dinner it was either cards or dressing-up. At Craven Lodge there was a party every week, and often these would be in fancy dress. The

The Marchioness of Blandford, the Marquess of Blandford, and Tommy McDougal.
The Blandfords hunted every season from Melton and leased the hunting estate of Lowesby.

The Jazz Band Group at a fancy-dress party at Craven Lodge held in February 1923.
Left to right, back row: Mrs Marge Harrison, the Hon. Gilbert Greenall, Mr Jack
Harrison, the Hon. Edward Greenall, unknown, the Hon Mrs Gilbert Greenall. Front row:
Sandra Crawford, Monica Sheriffe, Harry Cottrell, Mrs Sofer-Whitburn ('Tiddles').

Fancy dress at Craven Lodge. Miss Monica Sheriffe and the Hon. Mrs Fred (Violet) Cripps playing at being cats.

turn-out for the fancy dress could be sophisticated. A favourite amusement was to go in drag, and another was to dress as animals or circus figures. Ideas were exchanged rapidly. In one there was a jazz group whose musicians pre-date contemporary 'punk' by almost sixty years. The press gave the following description of the party when they dressed as schoolchildren:

> The ballroom was converted into a nursery, with nursery pictures and rhymes decorating the walls, and all the guests dressed as small children, and carried favourite toys. The hostess welcomed her guests dressed in a frilly frock of pale organdie muslin and hugging a Teddy bear. Captain Player wore a sailor suit. Captain Sam Ashton was Little Lord Fauntleroy in a velvet suit and with bare knees; Major Jack Harrison was an Eton boy; Lord Northland was a schoolgirl in a short red check frock and black curls; and Lady Brownlow, Lady Anne Bridgeman, the Hon. Mrs Edward Greenall, and Miss Monica Sheriffe were schoolgirls in party frocks, socks and corkscrew curls.

Lady Irene Curzon (later Baroness Ravensdale) at Craven Lodge, February 1924.

Miss Monica Sheriffe as a Twenties-style Pierrette and Mr Mike Wardell as a dairy maid, at Craven Lodge, 1924.

The Judges' wagon at the Belvoir point-to-point, 1923. Wearing a black bowler and overcoat is Captain Bertie Sheriffe. Next to him is Bobbie Clayton Swan talking to the Earl of Londesborough.

As Melton filled with hundreds of rich and demanding people, the hunting took on a different slant. Leicestershire had always had to entertain those whose main interest was in a fast run with plenty of jumping, but now the numbers were larger than ever. On the fashionable days the fields could count nearly 400, and they wanted to gallop. A professional huntsman had to know how to deal with this. If a run ended with the line gone, he would keep hounds running as if a fox was still there until he reached the next covert, when he would draw again. The majority of the field would not know what was happening and think that they were having an excellent time. It was the only way to manage followers who would have grumbled at once if there was not sufficient 'sport'.

But the bevy of larking socialites did not interfere with those who were genuine about their hunting. In those days without wire, you could jump a fence anywhere, the whole country was grass, and the field soon sorted itself out. There were also many who went superbly on equally superb mounts. But it was a test of horsmanship to be in front if you could not pay the top price for your hunters. Philip Cantrell-Hubbersty did not have the income of Ambrose Clarke or Sir Harold Nutting, and he had to look around for his horses, but it was agreed that he was 'the best man to hounds' in the country. He had grown up in the Shires, and apart from the interruption of war, he had hunted a five-day week every season. There was no life for Philip in Melton, and he was never seen at Craven Lodge. His evenings were devoted to

A Shires landscape between the wars. The Belvoir cubhunting, with a view across the famous vale.

hunting reflections in his study at Ragdale. To a visitor from another part of England there would only be one question, 'How's the sport?' He regarded the Quorn as his kingdom, to the frequent irritation of Harold Nutting. 'That bloody man . . .!' Nutting would yell, as Philip went off in his own direction taking half the field with him.

Some of those who went well and were noticed were neither rich nor landed. Reggie Hobbs was Master of the Horse to Ambrose Clarke, his job being to look after and school the fifty thoroughbred hunters. He was one of the few people whom

a huntsman could rely on to be always there and tell him which way a fox had gone. His son, Bruce, now a trainer, was educated in the art of horsemanship by his father, and went on to win the Grand National on Battleship at the age of seventeen. But to be a top man across country and to mix this with 'the arts' was unusual. Tommy Bouch was a rare exception. He was considered a brilliant man to hounds and he fancied himself as a poet. Hunting people could not quite make him out. He would go to Belvoir Castle and read his poems to Lady Diana Manners (later Cooper), a distinctly non-hunting person. Belvoir was referred to as 'the hothouse' by the

The Hon. Mrs Fred Cripps, one of the bravest lady riders across Leicestershire, has a day on foot. She watches a meet of the Quorn from her car, December 1926.

hunting crowd. It had, they believed, intellectual pretensions. None the less, if Bouch was not pursuing his quarry in the open, he was reading his verse to a tactful audience at the Castle.

In this competitive Shires' society women came forward as daring riders. Voted one of the best performers was Violet Cripps, a former wife of Bendor, 2nd Duke of Westminster. Whilst married to the Duke she had kept her own pack of harriers at Eaton Hall in Cheshire. She hunted and rode in point-to-points side-saddle, and often wore a velvet cap. It was not done then for women to wear caps, the headgear reserved for Masters, hunt servants and farmers, but she claimed that since she had been a Master in Cheshire she was entitled to do so. Violet Cripps was considered 'fun', but also tough and determined. Her sister hunted from Melton, too, and there had been a lifelong rivalry. The hunting accentuated it. It was said that they did not speak, even if they fell at the same fence.

The end of a fast run – and the exhaustion shows on a lady follower who might prefer to ride astride. Many women found that hunting side-saddle made their backs ache, but the side-saddle convention was not to go until the late Twenties.

Miss Monica Sheriffe, one of the daring Melton ladies, relieved to be astride at last.

The convention that many of the daring women wished to discard was riding side-saddle. Monica Sheriffe, whose family had lived and hunted in Leicestershire from before the war, was one of those outspoken ladies. She rated the discomfort of the side-saddle very high: 'Goodness, it was hell! Riding a mile down a road nearly broke one's back.' But the revolution was to take time. It began gently at first with a girl called 'Leixie' Wilson who came out in a divided skirt. Slowly, others followed until, in the season of 1928, the women rebelled. Those who wanted to, rode astride, and no one was going to send them home.

It was a fast society, and, between the hunting and the socialising, amorous activity was not neglected. Besides the Prince of Wales, there were several who were the objects of desire. A leader among ladies' men was Hugh Molyneux, later Lord Sefton. The Marahanee of Cooch Behar came all the way from India to woo him and took a lodge in Melton. She started to hunt and wore a habit. But the black of the habit and the erectness of the hunting seat clashed with her smooth, oriental poise, and the Meltonians thought it would have been wiser for her to have remained on foot and admired in a sari. Another Adonis was Tommy McDougal. With a gallant war record in the Scots Greys, and a dandy as a dresser, there were few who could resist him. He was known to have kept a mistress for some weeks one summer in a hunting spinney near Melton. The mistress slept on a lilo mattress and every day McDougal would ride out there, bringing her caviar and smoked salmon. And then there were the womanisers. Admiral Lord Beatty, for instance, a fine rider, was also proficient, it was rumoured, 'on the quarter deck'. These womanisers practised their charms with all the masculine excesses of the Edwardian mashers. It was an approach summed up by Algie Burnaby when he spoke of his preferred variety of theatrical entertainment, 'What I like to see is a pretty girl jumping through a hoop.'

Protected by its sport and high-living, Melton felt no pressures from an outside world. Even those who travelled up to hunt from London did not noticeably bear the the air of a profession. They might be younger sons who had secured a safe position in a bank or a firm of stockbrokers. But a job was still a secondary consideration when set against fulfilling the education of a country-house upbringing. Or if there was an occasional Member of Parliament, he did not arrive weary with last night's debate. The humdrum of the everyday was left behind. The contented values of the Meltonians were there to bring balm, but it was an enclosed society that knew each other's foibles and how to tease. Melton had its doggerel rhymster, Charlie Carlos Clarke, a good-looking wit who hunted and acted as gentleman-agent to the Marquis of Blandford at Lowesby. He directed his rhyming couplets at any quirk or indiscretion which turned into a talking point. An invariable topic was Lionel Tennyson's latest misdemeanour. Clare had now left Lionel, and Carlos Clarke composed the following piece of verse as 'A Welcome to Lord Tennyson on his Second Marriage':

When are you going to let me meet
This lady who is rich and sweet.
I long to see a woman who,
Could possibly have married you.

I hear you got a trifle tight
And told her that the Isle of Wight
Was peopled with a coloured race
And that you owned the bloody place.

You said you were a sort of King
Who signed a chit for everything,
A statement when applied to you,
We must admit is nearly true.

It's sad, the walls of Jermyn Street
Will cease to hear your running feet.
But all the Tarts are very glad,
You never paid the ones you had.

Give up, you old pot-bellied swine,
The hawking of indifferent wine,
Devote your life to make amends
To thousands of your thirsty friends.

But hunting in the cream of the Shires could be dangerous. On a good day it was possible to jump eighty or more fences and at each one there was — and still is — the element of risk. Many of the fences would be straightforward brush, but others might have a drop or the going might be bad, and, riding at speed, anything can happen. Out hunting, however, the danger is not considered and it was in the heroic image to be carried back on a gate with limbs broken. The usual breakage is the collar-bone, but legs and ribs are not infrequently crushed if a horse rolls on its rider when coming down. And worse than that, there can be death. In the Melton playground betweeen the wars Monica Sheriffe's sister, Joan, broke her neck after only six months of marriage, and Colonel Sam Ashton, a favourite of the Craven Lodge entertainments, was killed when his horse caught his foot in a rabbit hole.

It is essential that the hunt servants be well mounted and when Sir Harold Nutting came to the Quorn he gave his hunt servants the best horses available. The Shire packs were the preservers of efficiency, style and tradition, and throughout these decades no standard was allowed to slip. Nutting was appalled by anyone misusing hunting terminology. Cub-hunting was *not* 'cubbing' and a whipper-in was *not* 'a whip'. With the Belvoir it was Edward Greenall, the son of Sir Gilbert Greenall, now Lord Daresbury, who gave that pack the necessary attention and finance. The foundations had been solidly laid by Sir Gilbert and when his son took

"Cubbing P 122.

The Hon. Edward Greenall (later Lord Daresbury), Master of the Belvoir from 1935. Greenall was one of the best dressed hunting men in Melton. He was a popular Master, and is remembered to this day with affection by the farmers.

On the left, Major Guy Paget, who lived in the Pytchley country, taking a point-to-point fence alongside his son Reggie Paget (now the Labour Peer, Lord Paget).

the Mastership in the 1930s he showed himself to be an authority on hound-breeding, a natural horseman, and a valued friend to farmers. For hunting to be popular in a country, a close alliance between the Master and the farmer is important: it is by the latter's permission that a pack crosses much of the country (and increasingly so as estates are divided up). Edward Greenall was able to keep this alliance both respected and cherished.

Alongside the gossip and the parties went on the time-old duty of organising the sport – the visiting of farmers by the Masters or Hunt Secretaries, the arranging of meets and the repairing of damage caused by the followers. For the mending of timber a farmer might be given a supply of rails, although in the Shires this was less necessary as the blackthorn hedges were the natural fencing of the grazing cattle. But all the Masters of that period were aware of keeping the relationships in order, and the more so when there were several hundred society thrusters pounding over the land. The Masters called on the farmers regularly in their houses and had a friendship with them that was often more lasting than the friendships struck in the Melton night life. The farmers, they knew, would endure. Colonel Colman, when Master of the Belvoir, was quick to correct a socialite who had behaved ungratefully. For Philip Cantrell-Hubbersty the market place at Melton or Leicester was the homing ground where he knew ease.

For the other two Shire packs, the Fernie and the Pytchley, the social life remained more traditionally county. The hunting in both was grassland, but there was no local town like Melton which owed its existence to the chase. It was smart to hunt with either pack, although the Pytchley was perhaps an edge 'smarter'. The Fernie, in spite of being a bold and exciting country, was too close in competition to the packs round Melton, and in consequence suffered unfairly, whereas the Pytchley was far enough removed to hold its independence. The Pytchley, with its large grass fields and thick, thorn hedges with a ditch on one side, was still the toughest of the Shire countries to negotiate. A hunting country is determined by its agriculture, each area differing according to the type of grazing grass and the cattle suitable for it. In the Quorn area of Leicestershire the grazing was mainly dairy, and the fields therefore small, but Northamptonshire had some of the best grass for fattening bullocks, which were kept in large fields with thick upright hedges.

Frank Freeman continued to hunt the Pytchley through to his retirement in the middle Thirties. The Mastership now revolved around members of the Lowther family (kinsmen to the Yellow Earl), but an exception was Ronald Tree, a rich and intelligent American who had been raised in England and was to be instrumental in setting up the British War Relief Fund. Tree and his American wife, Nancy, did attempt to introduce something of the Melton image into a rather conservative Pytchley. From their house, Kelmarsh, they attracted hunting sophisticates who enjoyed charades and after-dinner games. But otherwise the Pytchley field was made up of hunting officers from Weedon, hard-riders and locals from either farms or country houses. For several seasons the Duke of York took a hunting-box there, preferring it to the social Melton. The followers might number 200 or so, but the Pytchley was not frivolous. The Lowthers were straightlaced hunting men and, for them, entertainment was restricted to the hunt ball.

But of the three strictly Melton countries it was the Cottesmore which had the reputation as the toughest to ride over. The Quorn had fences you could fly like a steeplechase but the Cottesmore was wild and untamed. It was of a run in the Cottesmore country that Bromley-Davenport had written in 'The Dream of an Old Meltonian':

> Oh! gently, my young one; the fence we are nearing
> Is leaning towards us — 'tis hairy and black,
> The binders are strong, and necessitate clearing,
> Or the wide ditch beyond will find room for your back.

His epic poem of the Member of Parliament falling asleep in the House to recall a fast burst across the Cottesmore county came to represent everything that the Shires stood for to hard-riding foxhunters. In those 'thirty bright minutes from Ranksboro' Gorse' was revealed the hunting man's philosophy. For the worthiest feat of all in the grass kingdoms was to be there at the finish, exhibiting as ever courage and initiative — the finest credentials a man could possess. The drowsing MP, brought back to reality by the dull drone of a debater, exhorts the descendants of those brave riding men to live by their stirling qualities:

> And oh! young descendants of ancient top-sawyers!
> By your lives to the world their example enforce;
> Whether landlords, or parsons, or statesmen, or lawyers,
> Ride straight as they rode it from Ranksboro' Gorse.

That spirit of bold performance was no less visible than in Mr Bromley-Davenport's day. The social life at Melton did not obscure it, and the two aspects of hunting in the Shires between the wars existed side by side. During the 1930s the Cottesmore was exceptional in that its Master hunted the hounds himself. Tommy Bouch occasionally hunted the Belvoir hounds, but it was not the custom in the Shires for a Master to hunt hounds. With the large fields, the pressures would have been too great for anyone who did not have professional training. But Chattie Hilton-Green disproved the rule. Hilton-Green, an Englishman with an army background, was brought up to hunting. He had come from the Cotswolds and with the Cottesmore he was to make a name as one of the outstanding amateur huntsmen of the age. And so there were still those who came to Leicestershire for no more than the splendour of the grass, the obstacles and the chase — single-minded sportsmen on whom so much of foxhunting rests.

The intake of visitors to Melton had provided a stimulus to local trade and farming at a badly needed moment. The Depression did not go unfelt there, but at least the farmers could sell their hay and corn to the hunting yards. For although Leicestershire was primarily a grass country, the odd stretches of high land were always ploughed. But it was light ploughing, not sown until March, and it did not interfere with the hunting. The horse-copers had a thriving industry with a continual turnover of stock to the yards. From Melton there was the demand for saddlery and boots, met by Hollinshead, the saddlers, and Rowell, the bootmakers. And if the hunting clothes were made mainly in London, there were the additional people to be fed — the multitude of seasonal visitors, guests and servants. Many of the lodges would have ten to twelve indoor servants, and the same number in the yards. In and around Melton there were about twenty lodges, not to mention the hunting-box estates like Baggrave and Lowesby nearby. This meant a constant supply of orders

The opening meet of the Belvoir at Croxton Park, November 1934. Left to right: Lady Daresbury, her grandson Master Edward Greenall, and his governess, Miss Webster.

A scene that brings back memories. Meltonians discussing yesterday's sport and last night's entertainment as they wait at covert-side. Second from the right is Major-General Vaughan, the owner and originator of Craven Lodge.

to victuallers, butchers, bakers and every variety of shop. At a time when the rural depression seemed eternal, Melton experienced a prosperity that surely could not end.

But the prosperity did end — and it came quickly, in 1939, with the declaration of another war. To those few who survive today and remember that hunting dream which had erupted so quickly from the ashes of the Great War, it is now hardly credible. The horses were once again requisitioned. The lodges emptied, the grooms, stablemen and servants went, and the rich departed. The white leather breeches, so laborious to clean but so warm and comfortable to wear, were never to return, and those expensive Savile Row habits were to be cut up by some as wartime clothing. Waiting each day for the blackout, a deserted Melton was like a town of ghosts. The clatter of a hundred horses and the laughter from Craven Lodge had already receded into the past. And even the press cuttings which had chronicled the daily sport and nightly gaiety appeared dated.

6
Sport to Come Home to

With a nation at war, hunting was again under threat. It was the policy of the wartime government that hunting be carried on wherever possible to control the fox population, but similar problems were to confront hunts as before in the Great War – lack of men and horses, reducing of packs, and rationing of petrol and food. And with the blackout the hunting started earlier and the days were shorter. But it did continue, even if certain packs had to be managed single-handed. The Lanarkshire and Renfrewshire over the Border was run entirely by the huntsman, William Dickinson, who continued to hunt them twice a week, and one man alone organised the Ludlow. In the Shires, the Quorn, Belvoir and Cottesmore were kept in existence by their huntsmen and by Philip Cantrell-Hubbersty, Edward Greenall and Lady Helena Fitzwilliam respectively. Every Saturday night, as the bombs fell, these three would telephone each other and discuss the sport of the week.

That the sport did not die was more than ever due to the farmers. Wherever food could be spared it was sent to the kennels. The farmers gave animal carcases unfit for human consumption, and if a pack was about to fold, it was generally the farmers who rescued it. For the farmers' situation had improved since the outbreak of war. As German U-boats successfully sank merchant shipping carrying imported goods, England was to find herself thrown back on her own resources. But as the agriculture of the country had been largely neglected by the governments of the 1930s, Britain was by no means self-sufficient. Faced with the possibility of starvation the Government now rallied to the farmers. Direct subsidies were granted, Agricultural Committees set up in each county, and the farmers encouraged to produce foodstuffs to keep the nation and her armies alive. Overnight, the farmer became a most important person. 'A Farmer is Worth a Brigadier,' went one newspaper heading.

Nor had the serving soldier lost his keenness to hunt. At the outbreak of war mounted cavalry regiments were posted abroad to Palestine. The detachment consisted of the 1st Cavalry Division and all the yeomanry regiments. The horses were

Cavalry horses from London let loose at the Melton Remount Depot and seeing grass for the first time.

Melton Mowbray was the only Remount Depot during the Second World War. The remount girls prepare to saddle up for morning exercise.

The Hon. Diana Holland-Hibbert no longer hunting, but driving her truck as a Corporal in the Auxiliary Territorial Service, 1940.

In the centre is Brigadier 'Boy' Selby Lowndes with some of his Lille Beagles. He hunted them in France during the 'phoney' war, but they had to be destroyed at the retreat from Dunkirk.

made up of the black cavalry chargers and requisitioned hunters, and they numbered around 20,000. They had been sent there at first to keep the peace between the Jews and the Arabs and to maintain a British influence in the Middle East. But there were long periods of inaction, during which many hunted. English foxhounds were drafted from home and from a pack near Baghdad, and with them the cavalry hunted not the fox, but the jackal. But it was short-lived. By 1942, most of the cavalry had been transferred to armoured cars. And yet it did not stop a Selby Lowndes from forming a pack of beagles in Northern France and hunting them consistently throughout the 'phoney' war of 1939–40. But with the retreat to Dunkirk this hunting venture had to end, too.

On leave, the soldiers could find the hunting there as always, but the hunting landscape was changing as never before. An instruction from the Government was

*Major Philip Cantrell-Hubbersty, one of Leicestershire's boldest riders,
Master of the Quorn and determined that hunting should continue,
in spite of war.*

The post-war recovery. Colonel G. A. Murray-Smith (right back) riding in the Leicestershire Yeomanry race at the Meynell point-to-point, 1946. The camera catches one competitor just as he is about to fall.

that land be ploughed to produce the quantities of potatoes, corn and sugar beet, which formed the nation's diet. Those farmers staffing the Agricultural Committees had a duty to advise other farmers what land must be ploughed, and by the end of the war several million acres had reverted to plough. There was even plough in the Shires and the elderly hunting men predicted that the sport could not be the same. But hunting has untapped sources of resilience. Long ago, Hugo Meynell had said at the end of his reign, 'Hunting can't last another ten years.' And now, in spite of a further five years of European war, there was still what Cantrell-Hubbersty insisted there should be when he took over the Quorn, namely 'Sport to come home to.'

Following the war, the packs were quick to reshape themselves and return to their accustomed strength. In the post-war years the risk to foxhunting was not seen to be so much a matter of finance or altered farming as an increased hearing given to the anti-blood sports lobby. A Private Member's Bill was introduced in the House to make illegal the hunting of deer, otter or badger, and the coursing of hares and rabbits. With a House that had a Labour majority, 392 Labour Members to 216 Conservatives, the Bill was defeated by 214 votes to 101. A subsequent Bill which would have illegalized foxhunting was withdrawn, but the Government undertook to appoint a Committee to enquire into and report on the question of cruelty to wild animals. Having made a full enquiry into every aspect of hunting the fox, the report stated 'that hunting should be allowed to continue'. The 1949 Scott Henderson enquiry was the most comprehensive study ever carried out, and in it are answered finally the questions that abolitionists repeatedly raise.

If hunting was safe from the the anti-blood sports lobby it was to be made more difficult by a definite shift in the county framework. The collapse of large estates

Mr Winston Churchill, out for a day with the Old Surrey and Burstow in 1949, and hunting in protest at the proposal to ban the sport.

which had first been evident in the 1920s was now widespread. Death duties, two agricultural depressions and the depreciating value of money had at last weakened many county magnates. It was a situation feared and foreseen years before by Lord Willoughby de Broke when he had spoken of Radicals attacking the values of the countryside by the curbing of landed power and thereby laying their hands 'on the very Ark of the Covenant in the shape of the hereditary principle'. The imposition of the Death Duty Tax had been a Liberal measure, and the countryside blamed first the Radicals and later the Labour attitude for the gravity of both depressions. The effect on hunting was that many more old county families could no longer support packs of hounds, and not every rich man taking up country residence had the sympathy and understanding of a Mr Brassey. The traditions and standards of the sport were in danger of being lost.

The support of the farmers became vital, for as more estates were sold off, so there were more independent farmers. But the farmers had proved their devotion in the last war, and when the ban on cruel sports was under discussion it was the farmers who had formed together and ridden down Piccadilly in protest. In many respects the support of both tenant and independent farmers became the true justification of the popularity of hunting. For almost gone were the days when it could be written into a tenant's lease that he must permit the hunt to cross his land and that he must walk a foxhound puppy. The farmers, however, willingly continued to co-operate in each case. And as the county structure adapted it was not uncommon for farmers to be Masters.

By the 1950s the kind of person who hunted broadened again. This might have distressed the hall porter of the club in St James's who, when receiving an inquiry for a gentleman, cut in, 'A Gentleman, sir? There hasn't been a gentleman in here since 1914,' but it showed the flexibility of the hunting field. In a lot of packs tradespeople and businessmen from a nearby town would now vastly outnumber the gentry. But in those Shire packs, or the Beaufort, or the Heythrop, where the gentry still predominated they were expected to pay a rather higher subscription than they might have done before. Once, Masters paid for nearly three-quarters of the running cost, but now it was accepted that the burden be more evenly spread. The Quorn had cost Sir Harold Nutting around £15,000 a year. And there were very few left like Lord Leconfield, at Petworth, who had kennelled and paid for the hunt there from the turn of the century to the war.

The passing of Lord Leconfield in 1952 could indeed be taken to signify almost the end of an era for the great foxhunting autocrats, built in the nineteenth-century mould. He had lived all his life at Petworth where his ancestors before him had hunted the fox, and that blood had stayed in his veins. In early days he had hunted his hounds himself and even in old age he rarely left his huntsman's side. 'Draw, hounds, draw; otherwise I shall cut you in half!' he was heard to shout, in what was nearly his last season, at some hounds that were idling outside a covert. 'Then Your

The mainstay of hunting. Supporting Gloucestershire farmers in the 1950s.

Lordship will have two packs of hounds, will you not?' replied a trusted family retainer. Lord Leconfield had become known as a character, with an outlook quite his own. Hunting his pack one day in 1940, he was distressed to have his sport interrupted by a game of football. Standing high in his stirrups, he yelled across the pitch, 'Haven't you people got anything better to do in wartime than play *football?*' And his dying words had been on hunting, too. Turning to his heir, John Wyndham, he had inquired if he could blow a horn. The reply was, no, at least not well. 'If you weren't so bloody blind, you might make a bloody good huntsman: I can't stand a huntsman who makes a continual noise on his horn,' returned Lord Leconfield. After that, he expired.

What county families remained tended not to hunt so much as shoot. It was a change of fashion partly dictated by the expense of maintaining a stable of hunters. If you went for a week-end to a country-house there would not automatically be a horse to hunt on. But the fashion for shooting revived a difference between the two sports which had existed for a long time, and now came to a fresh head. Shooting estates did not want their coverts drawn until the end of their season in February. The argument, which was reinforced by the gamekeepers, was that the hounds disturbed the birds and that it took weeks to get them back. Rather than let the hunt kill the foxes, it was rumoured that they were shot or trapped. To shoot or trap a fox is an unpardonable breach of the sportsman's code, and back in the nineteenth century such conduct had inspired the following lines from the hunting poet, Egerton Warburton:

Captain Ronnie Wallace as Master of the Cotswold in the late 1940s. He was to set an example of maintaining standards in the post-war years.

> We hold in abhorrence all vulpicide knaves,
> With their gins, and their traps, and their velveteen slaves;
> They may feed their fat pheasants, their foxes destroy,
> And mar the prime sport they themselves can't enjoy;
> But such sportsmen as these we good fellows condemn,
> And I vow we'll ne'er drink a quaesitum to them.

The foxhunters argue that it does good rather than harm to draw shooting coverts regularly, and that, if anything, it encourages the fattening pheasants to fly and is an excellent preparation for a forthcoming shoot. A hunt never draws a covert in the afternoon as this could prevent the birds from returning to roost, and a covert would not be drawn less than a week before a shoot takes place. But shooting estates that have no interest in hunting do not listen to this argument, and there is often the complaint that when the hunt does come in February, the hounds never find a fox. Since the foxes have possibly been controlled by other methods, this is an unfair implication. Common sense would suggest that, with a little care and thought, the two sports can easily exist side by side without interference with each other.

The trusted give-and-take of relationships so important to the well-being of the countryside was no longer a matter of course. And if hunting was to ensure against criticism, it was all the more necessary that standards be maintained. Should the sport become slip-shod and untidy, its days would surely be numbered. All over the country new types of Masters were taking hounds who were sometimes unaware of the sport's honourable past. It was with this in mind that Captain Ronnie Wallace came to the front as a new and young Master who cared passionately about the preservation of standards and tradition. As a boy he had grown up in Sussex, hunting with the Eridge. It was a hunting background not unlike that of Siegfried Sassoon. His childhood was spent listening to the stories of grooms and learning from days in the kennels how the sport must operate. He was fortunate in having as an early mentor the Eridge huntsman, Will Freeman, brother of the more famous Frank. Will Freeman was also a first-class huntsman and a guardian of hunting standards. Once, in these post-war years, in his retirement, he had seen a hunt servant smoking at a point-to-point while in his uniform of office. Freeman had gone straight up to him and knocked the cigarette from his hand. It was this kind of dedication to duty that Ronnie Wallace so admired.

During his twenty-five years as Master of the Heythrop, Wallace preserved a pre-war hunting scene. Every farmer was carefully consulted and their problems discussed, and he earned their admiration as a single-minded sportsman and country-man in days when such enthusiasm in a young person appeared to be passing. The wearing of correct hunting clothes was also as important, and he liked to point out that riding over the land of others makes the field a guest, and a guest does not go out to dinner improperly dressed. He hunted a four-day week, usually hunting the hounds himself, and became a noted hound-breeder. When hunting ended in March, he would take the hounds down to Exmoor and hunt them there until May. He gave the Heythrop a style similar to that enjoyed by the Shire packs in the Golden Age. The followers numbered around 200 which was considerable for the 1950s and 1960s, and everyone spoke of the Heythrop with the excitement that surrounds the Quorn or the Belvoir. At a time when hunting might have drifted into a backwater, Ronnie Wallace generated a fresh optimism.

But an aspect of hunting which could never be retrieved was the change in terrain. With the lesson of two world wars, the country did not want to find itself with inadequate supplies on a third occasion, and the farmers continued to be encouraged with subsidies to keep the land under plough. Even the grass countries were effected, and as the Fifties turned to the Sixties, the aggravation of the plough increased year by year. Car followers increased, too, and those who had known hunting before the war now said that it could not go on. But the hunting did not stop; to suit the different landscape it adapted. As farm machinery improved, the ploughing was deeper, and with farms turning to mechanisation the number of men employed decreased. Fences were no longer cut and laid with the former skill and the use of wire had intensified as a labour-saving economy. For those packs which wanted to introduce Welsh blood to cope with new, scenting hazards, as a result of mechanisation, the Stud Book ruling was relaxed. And where wire was too extensive in a country to take down, the hunts erected their jumps. Yet if the landscape did not end hunting, there were claims that the expense would. But as the years went on, and the costs rose, more and more subscribers came out. The continuation of hunting was to surprise even its most fervent protagonists.

The bed-rock of the county had indeed been shaken, but it had not quite gone. The unity of the land and its hierarchy may have been disrupted by a redistribution of wealth, but the status of the farmer had improved, while the number of outsiders had increased. A bureaucratic officialdom might be replacing a feudal organisation of the county, yet the landlords still occupied their place of honour. Where it was possible, the farmers and the hunt looked first to them.

In Staffordshire, Mrs Inge of Thorpe Hall continued to dispense hospitality to the Atherstone. Hunting well into her eighties (although no longer Master), she was regarded as 'the mother of the hunt', and she had not lost an inch of style since Sassoon first described her. A boundless generosity overflowed from Thorpe to all who hunted and the county. When she came to die in the early Sixties she left in her

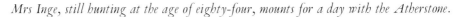

Mrs Inge, still hunting at the age of eighty-four, mounts for a day with the Atherstone.

The Pony Club Hunter Trials of the Chiddingfold and Leconfield in the 1960s. Children from varied backgrounds were ever more strongly taking to hunting through the Pony Club.

will that food and drink be ready in the dining-room on days that the hunt might be nearby. In Wales, a Sir Watkin Williams-Wynn was still 'uncrowned King' of North Wales on his large estates, and had returned as Master of the Wynnstay. In Lincoln-shire, Lord Yarborough governed vast acres and the Brocklesby with the family's traditional benevolent despotism. And though not a hunting man, to this day he pays for many of the pack's outgoings, and concerns himself with the hound-breeding. His estate is one of the few which maintains the custom in its tenants' leases that wire be taken down at the start of every season, and that the tenants walk a foxhound puppy.

Throughout the country bastions of hunting life remained. The Duke of Beaufort at Badminton and the Duke of Northumberland with the Percy — two packs which remained kennelled on their Master's estates. In Gloucestershire, the Berkeleys were hunting their hounds from Berkeley Castle as they had done for centuries. Certain ancient frameworks had withstood the various changes, but hunting had also taken a necessary levelling out. Impressive as some names might stand on paper, the sport was requiring finance from every quarter. By the Sixties each pack had its hunt supporters' association, raising funds from the foot- and carfollowers. The hunt balls were no longer exclusive dances for the resident gentry and their guests. Anyone who could buy a ticket was welcome and so, as they ceased to happen in country houses, they lost their exclusive value. But the core of the hunting fraternity recognised the importance of the levelling. As far back as the Fifties, Phyllis Cantrell-Hubbersty had suggested that a kind and rich farmer, Mr Fred Mee, join her in the Mastership. The Quorn had never known a farmer as Master, but it was by such adjustments that foxhunting was to preserve itself. What concerned every countryman was that the sport be there.

7

A Sun that Does not Set

One hundred years have passed since the Golden Age of foxhunting. However, there has always been an argument among the recorders of hunting history as to which was the true Golden Age of the nineteenth century. Many will say it was the period from 1840 to 1870 when land was enclosed and benefiting from drainage, there were no railroads, the country landlord was prosperous, the Radical measures were not yet felt, and the countryside was free from outside interference. The effects of the Industrial Revolution had not disturbed the peace of the countryman. Lord Willoughby de Broke, the spokesman for the rights of a country society, recognised that calm in the hunting paintings of Sir Francis Grant. The anxiety that the spread of Radicalism was to bring had not then settled on the brow of the country gentleman: 'There is no suggestion of neurasthenia in the pictures of Sir Francis Grant. He groups and paints those men who met the Foxhounds in the morning to ride over each other's land, and met together in the evening to drink each other's claret, as possessing an air of assurance, a power of command, a sense of property, a solidity of position, a freedom from worry, a distinction of manner, and a solemn, almost stodgy simplicity, which in those days must have been the characteristics of the gentlemen who were sportsmen as well as men of substance.'

And yet the Golden Age of 1870 to 1914, as depicted in this book, is considered by as many to be the great foxhunting epoch. The advantage of grass, despite a depression, and of those direct improvements brought about by the machine age, such as clipping and the better shoeing of horses, may have tipped the balance in favour of the latter epoch. Admittedly, wire became a fresh issue in the 1860s, but it was not yet the hindrance to riders that it became later. Hunting landlords either did not permit wire or requested that it be taken down at the start of the season. And it was viewed with dislike by most landlords and often had the reverse result of encouraging more perfect fencing. Estates were still large and the rich outsiders taking to the sport did so with an extravagance that exceeded their rural predecessors. Although by 1900 there existed the Death Duty tax and Income Tax, both were

But with the Great War that confidence was shaken. The economy was devastated, a revolution had occurred in Russia, and in Britain a socialist party would small and not thought to be serious. The destructive intentions of the Liberals and Mr Lloyd George were discussed in the country drawing-rooms but it was not believed that they could really put into jeopardy the sanctity of the English county. The divisions within the county were backed by the precedence of history, and binding the country classes together were not only ancient loyalties, but the pleasure of foxhunting.

The Queen with the Beaufort hounds at Badminton. On her left is Lady Sarah Armstrong-Jones and on her right, Prince Edward. Behind them is the Duke of Beaufort.

The scene does not alter. Charles Parker, the terrier man to the Heythrop during the Mastership of Ronnie Wallace, with his assistant.

The Berkeley moving off in their 1981 season with Berkeley Castle in the background. The Berkeley family have been hunting hounds for centuries, and the setting has not changed.

soon be in power. From the cities there spread the consciousness of class. The higher taxation was firmly directed at privilege and the landed came under attack. And as if increased taxation was not enough, the Depression of the 1930s struck. The destruction of the landed estate and the county unit had begun. But through it all, the farming gentry kept its confidence and determination. For hardly a pack of foxhounds disappeared, the three or four days a week of hunting did not lessen, and, ironically, the popularity of the sport broadened. By contrast, estates were sold, farmers bankrupted and the countryside almost abandoned to weed. But the hunting and its dependent events − the point-to-point, hunter trials, and the Pony Club gymkhana − continued. The permanence of hunting in a decade of black despair also brought security to those who lived by the land. For the farmer, landlord or tenant, hunting preserved their faith in a failing countryside.

That spirit from the Golden Age lasted into the 1950s. A decade later and the old-fashioned hunting gentry had almost gone, numerous country houses had been demolished and new people from the towns had come to live in the country, indifferent to many of the county traditions. Agriculture had improved, but the land was no longer suitable for the best conditions of hunting. Plough slowed down the pace and fertilisers damaged scenting, and yet once again the keenness to hunt rose above these drawbacks. By the 1970s wide strips of motorway had become familiar blots on not a few hunting landscapes. How could hounds be prevented from running across them and risking accidents? Coverts too close to motorways had to be given up, but the hunting continued.

Those fears raised at the arrival of the motor-car were slight by comparison with the disadvantages which were to follow, particularly since the last war, when neither urban nor farming progress has favoured the sport. An abundance of yellow lamplights, indicating fresh suburbs, now encircle at dusk a quantity of hunting horizons; and for the farmer the growing of winter corn has made his position difficult. With crops sown as early as October, he might prefer that horses did not gallop even round the edges of his fields, for carelessness from riders can soon cause damage. But hunting lies deep in the very bones of the countryman and to surrender it would be to halt the pulse of rural life. The majority of the farmers will still lend their support, and where the gentry have been obliged to leave, there is usually a farmer willing and rich enough to come to the aid of a pack. Today there is no other institution that reminds us so well of the harmony that was once the spirit of England's counties.

It is said that a wider cross-section of the community is now hunting than ever before. To reflect too much over what has changed can make for a loss of proportion. In many different places from the North to the West of England, good hunting is to be found. And some areas like North Wales, for the Wynnstay, and Derbyshire, for the Meynell, remain grass. There is grass still in Leicestershire, with unbroken stretches where a fast run, reminiscent of the Twenties, can be enjoyed. And the variety of hunting offered by the English countryside has not vanished. From the grass and blackthorn of the Shires, to the hill hunting in the Cotswolds and on Exmoor, to the dykes of East Yorkshire — there is still choice. Of course, there will always be the elderly who look disconsolately at their boots, shake their heads, and, turning to one another, say, 'I know it's been said before, but we've seen the best of it.' It is the remark made by each passing generation of foxhunters; and, as we know, it had been said 250 years before, by Hugo Meynell.

Though thorns be thick, though binders lace,
Though stout be stile and rail,
Though nought but blood can live the pace,
And nought but pluck prevail,
The call's to all, the field is fair
To every creed and class;
So draw your girths, all ye who dare,
And ride the English grass!

W. H. OGILVIE

Index

Numbers in italic indicate an illustration